BEST-EVER COOK'S COLLECTION

VEGETARIAN

BEST-EVER COOK'S COLLECTION

VEGETARIAN

THE DEFINITIVE COOK'S COLLECTION: OVER 200 STEP-BY-STEP VEGETARIAN RECIPES

Roz Denny

P

PARRAGON

This edition published in 1998 by
Parragon
Units 13-17, Avonbridge Trading Estate
Atlantic Road, Avonmouth
Bristol BS11 9QD

© Anness Publishing Limited 1994

Produced by
Anness Publishing Limited
Hermes House
88-89 Blackfriars Road
London SE1 8HA

ISBN 0-7525-2369-4 (hardback)
ISBN 0-7525-2372-4 (paperback)

Printed and bound in Italy

3 5 7 9 10 8 6 4 2

 THE LEAF SYMBOL NEXT TO A RECIPE INDICATES THAT IT IS SUITABLE FOR VEGANS.

Please note that mushroom ketchup may be used as a vegetarian substitute for Worcestershire sauce.
Anchovy essence may also be omitted from recipes.

MEASUREMENTS

Three sets of equivalent measurements have been provided in the recipes here, in the following order:
Metric, Imperial and American.
It is essential that units of measurement are not mixed within each recipe.
Where conversions result in awkward numbers, these have been rounded for convenience,
but are accurate enough to produce successful results.

CONTENTS

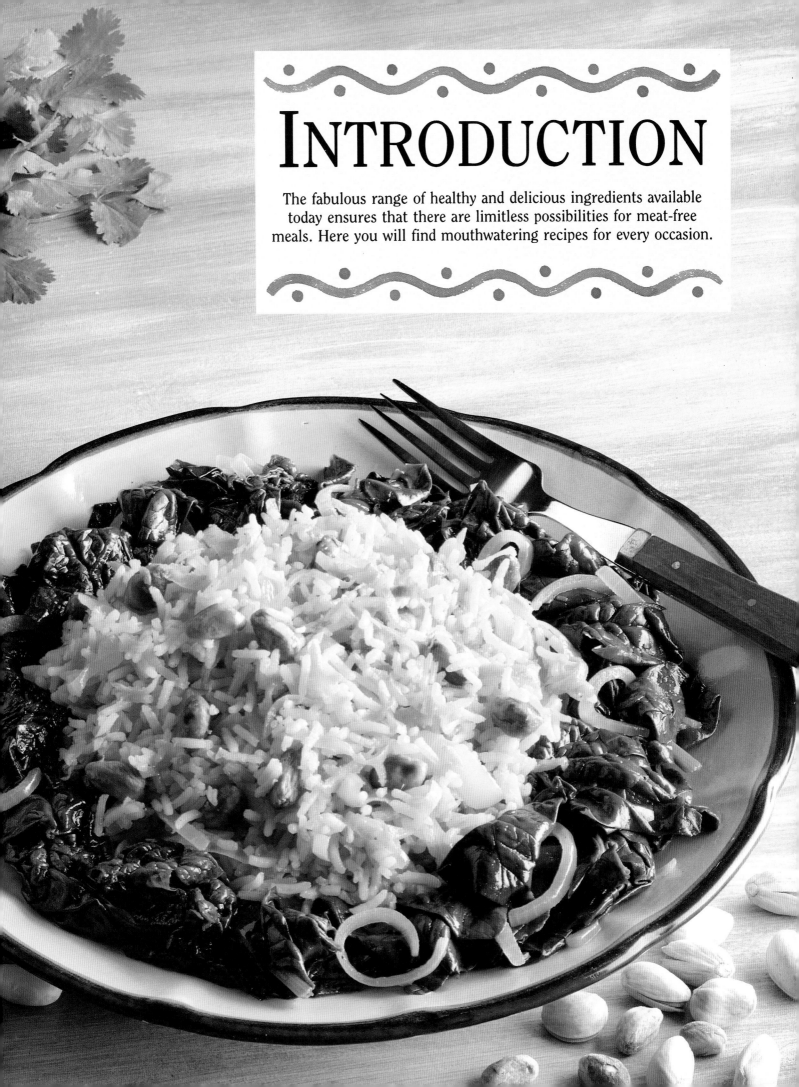

INTRODUCTION

The fabulous range of healthy and delicious ingredients available today ensures that there are limitless possibilities for meat-free meals. Here you will find mouthwatering recipes for every occasion.

Introduction

The human body needs certain nutrients if it is to remain in perfect working order, to be fully effective, and alert, to keep energy levels high and resistance to illness strong, to help young bodies grow and for older bodies to get the most from life.

The human being is naturally omnivorous, in that the body can digest a wide range of foods. But it also has a discerning and intelligent brain enabling it to make different choices. For an increasing number of people in the Western world, the choice is being made to eat flesh-free meals, consuming foods that do not contain animal products or cause animals suffering or death.

The growth of vegetarianism in the West, through choice rather than necessity or religious beliefs, has focused our attention on the tremendous attractiveness of meat-free dishes. We have discovered the joy of cooking with foods such as grains, pulses and vegetables. We begin to appreciate the sheer beauty of the colours, shapes and textures of these foods. It has made many of us look again at our diets and methods of cooking.

So, this book is written not just for those converted to the virtues of vegetarianism, but is also intended to tempt 'omnivores' to the vegetarian way of eating and to show that it is possible to produce a delicious and attractive meal, free from the tyranny of the 'meat and two veg' way of menu planning.

The ideal well-balanced diet is one that contains sufficient levels of calories, proteins, carbohydrates, fats, vitamins and minerals. No one food contains all the nutrients we need, although some contain more than others and some vitamins can only be obtained easily through animal products. The secret for eating a well-balanced, healthy diet is to eat a wide variety of foods to ensure you include all the nutrients you need. A few likes and dislikes may not cause problems, but too many fads may mean you are not taking all the nutrients your body needs.

So the golden rule that nutritionists and doctors ask us to practise is to eat all foods in moderation and to eat a great variety of foods. This variety is especially important for vegetarians; the occasional indulgence is fine, but too much of one or two foodstuffs (especially fats) could cause health problems.

Because vegetarians eat more grains, vegetables, pulses and fruit in their diet than meat eaters, they seem to obtain a greater amount of dietary fibre, or as it is now known NSP (non-starch polysaccharides). However, they have to be careful not to increase their intake of high fat dairy products such as cheese, butter and cream. Just like meat eaters, they should watch their intake of these potentially high cholesterol products. Where possible choose lower fat versions. There are an increasing number on the market which are usually well labelled. Changing from full fat milk to skimmed or semi-skimmed milk helps, as does eating plenty of low fat yogurts, fromage frais and skimmed milk soft cheeses.

Iron can also be a particular problem for vegetarians if they are not aware of the sources from which it can be obtained. Also, iron from vegetable sources cannot be utilized by the body unless there is vitamin C present in the same meal to act as a catalyst. But a small piece of fruit, fresh salad or even a good squeeze of lemon juice soon redresses that problem.

Vegans (those who exclude dairy products from their diet) need to ensure they take in sufficient calcium either in the form of calcium tablets or calcium enriched soya milk. They may also need to supplement their diet with other vitamins such as Vitamin B2 (riboflavin) and B12 and minerals such as iodine, which can be obtained simply by using iodized salt. A vegan diet can be just as healthy as a well-balanced omnivorous diet, so long as followers are well informed about suitable foods.

AIM TO EAT EACH DAY

A GOOD SELECTION FROM EACH

OF THESE CATEGORIES

☐ Grains, including pasta, rice (brown and white), oats (including porridge), barley, quinoa and high fibre breakfast cereals or crispbreads

☐ Breads and potatoes, cooked with the minimum of oil, butter or cream

☐ Pulses and legumes such as lentils, kidney beans, split peas, aduki beans etc.

☐ Plenty of fresh vegetables, especially leafy greens like spinach, and fresh fruits

☐ Low fat natural/unsweetened yogurt, skimmed milk soft cheese/quark, fromage frais

☐ Moderate amounts of dried fruits (apricots, prunes, raisins etc.) and unsalted nuts (peanuts, almonds, walnuts, hazelnuts etc.)

☐ Cautious amounts of cheese, especially high fat types

☐ Cautious amounts of oils, margarines, butter and cream

☐ Occasional cautious amounts of processed foods with high 'hidden fats' such as biscuits, cakes, crisps, pastry goods

THE VEGETARIAN LARDER

The starchy foods

Nutritionists and doctors are now encouraging us all to eat a great deal more of complex carbohydrate foods, which is great news for vegetarians and all creative cooks, as these foodstuffs are all so versatile, nourishing and – best of all – cheap. They also store well without refrigeration and can be cooked with the minimum of preparation. Starchy foods have reasonable amounts of protein plus vitamins from the B group and minerals such as phosphorous, zinc, iron, potassium and, in the case of bread, added calcium. The other main advantage is they are good sources of dietary fibre (NSP).

Flours

Have a selection of different flours to ring the changes. Often it is a good idea to mix two types together in baking for flavour and texture. Use half wholemeal and half plain white flours for a lighter brown pastry crust or bread loaf. Mix buckwheat flour with plain white for pancakes and so on. Flour is a good source of protein as well as complex starchy carbohydrate, and indispensable in cooking. If you don't buy flour often, buy it in small amounts and store in an airtight container.

Brown/wholemeal flours as well as buckwheat have a shorter shelf life than the more refined types of white flours. Remember too, that self-raising flours with their added raising agent lose their lightening ability after about six months.

Rice

There is an increasingly attractive range to choose from. Ideally, avoid easy-cook rice as this has a chewy texture and much of the natural flavour processed out of it. The pre-steaming process does mean, however, that marginally more of the water soluble vitamins and minerals are retained.

Top of the rice range is basmati, an elegant, fragrant, long grain rice grown in the foothills of the Himalayas. Traditionally eaten with curries, basmati is marvellous in almost all dishes, sweet and savoury, especially pilaffs. Brown basmati is a lighter wholegrain rice with higher levels of dietary fibre. Thai rices are delicate and lightly sticky and are particularly good in stir-fries and wonderful in milk puddings. Wild rice (not a real rice, but an aquatic grass) has good levels of proteins. Pre-soaking shortens the cooking time.

Pasta

The mainstay of many a cook in a hurry. Again, a good source of starchy complex carbohydrates. Available in a multitude of shapes, colours and now even flavours. Good pasta should cook to a tender texture but retain a firm bite, which the Italians call *al dente* (to the tooth). For this, choose pasta that is made with durum wheat or durum semolina. Cook pasta in plenty of boiling salted water according to the instructions on the pack, then drain, rinse in cold water and shake lightly. Italians serve pasta slightly wet. Return to the pan with some olive oil, seasoning and a grating of fresh nutmeg.

Wholewheat pastas have a more nutty flavour and chewy texture. They are particularly good in creamy sauces such as macaroni cheese. Choose pasta shapes to match the sauce. Long thin pasta such as linguine and spaghetti are best served with light thin sauces; shells and tubes are complemented well by creamy and rich sauces.

Potatoes

Like rice, potatoes are beginning to enjoy something of a culinary renaissance as more cooks realize that choosing the right variety for a dish is one secret of success. Also, more potatoes are being grown for flavour and are often delicious served simply boiled in their skins lightly dressed with a little olive oil or butter. Choose small waxy firm potatoes for salads, larger firm ones for roasting, and floury varieties for mashing. More and more producers are printing suitable uses on the bags, so check these first.

Pulses

Over half the world's main source of protein comes from pulses in one form or another. However, although high in protein, pulses are not complete in all amino acids. In particular they lack one of the amino acids called methionine. Grain foods on the other hand lack lysine and tryotophan, which pulses do have. But, put them together and you have completed the usual protein circle. So, when you eat any pulses try to include starches in the same meal, such as lentils with rice, houmous with bread, beans with pasta and so on. In addition include some fresh vitamin C in the meal (from fruits or leafy vegetables) so that your body can utilize the iron in the grains and pulses.

The variety of pulses is exciting and seemingly endless. Dried pulses benefit from soaking, preferably overnight. Older pulses may need longer. To shorten soaking time, cover with boiling water and leave for 2 hours. Drain and boil in fresh water. Boil pulses fast for the first 10 minutes of cooking to destroy any potential mild toxins present. Then lower the heat and gently simmer. Do not add salt or lemon juice during cooking as this toughens the skins, although fresh herbs and onion slices add flavour. Like pasta, don't overdrain. Leave wet. Season and maybe dress with extra virgin olive oil.

Certain lentils can be cooked without pre-soaking. The small split red lentils (or Masoor Dhal) are marvellous for sprinkling in as thickeners for soups and stews and take just 20 minutes to cook. Beans with a good creamy texture that is perfect for soups, patés and purées are butter beans, kidney beans (red and black), cannellini, haricots, borlotti, pinto beans and flageolets. Split peas and red lentils make marvellous dips. Chick peas and aduki beans hold their texture well and make a good base for burgers and stews.

Fats and oils

For general frying, choose oils high in polyunsaturates. Sunflower, rape seed and groundnut have the lightest flavours and these are the ones preferred by gourmet cooks. Corn oil and blended vegetable oils are stronger in flavour. Increasingly popular is olive oil. Not only highly prized for flavour, it also has properties beneficial to health, being high in monosaturates which are thought to help reduce blood cholesterol levels. Two main qualities are available – pure olive oil, excellent for general cooking, and extra virgin oil made from the first cold pressing of the olives, producing a full-flavoured, almost peppery taste, ideal for dressing salads and as a healthier flavour substitute for butter. Aromatic seed and nut oils (e.g. sesame, walnut and hazelnut) are too heavy and expensive for general use, but they are ideal for trickling on hot vegetables, pulses or pasta. Store these aromatic oils in the fridge. Others are fine kept at room temperature.

All fats, unless labelled specifically 'lower' or 'reduced fat' contain approximately the same amount of calories. It is the type of fat within them that counts healthwise. Sunflower and olive oil spreads are lower in harmful saturates and higher in healthier polyunsaturates and monosaturates. Spreads labelled 'low fat' or 'reduced fat' will have more added water which helps reduce the calories, but also makes them more difficult for frying and baking.

Fats and oils are important in our diets, contributing vital vitamins such as A, D and E, so do not cut them out altogether. Include them in moderate amounts. Check pack labels for full nutritional details and remember to restrict your fat intake to no more than a third of your total daily intake of calories.

Cheese

A popular high protein food with vegetarians, cheese is also high in calories, having twice the number of many carbohydrate and protein foods. For fuller flavour choose well matured varieties of cheese such as a mature farmhouse Cheddar or fresh Parmesan – you will then not need to use as much.

Many vegetarians seek out cheeses made with vegetarian rennet and more of the popular cheeses are made this way.

For cooking, choose mature cheeses. I like to leave some full flavoured cheeses unwrapped in the refrigerator to dry out – this concentrates the flavour and makes them go further when finely grated.

Lower fat cheeses are often not as full flavoured as normal varieties and the temptation is to use more of them, which rather counteracts their purpose!

My favourite cheeses are fully mature Cheddar, fresh Parmesan, mature Gruyère and Pecorino – an Italian sheeps' cheese. Lower fat soft cheeses and goats' cheeses are ideal for stirring into hot food to make an instant, tasty creamy sauce.

Dairy products

Supermarket chiller cabinets carry a great range of cultured dairy goods which present many exciting opportunities for the home cook. Crème frâiche is a French-style soured cream which does not curdle when boiled, so it is ideal stirred into hot dishes. It will also whip, adding a light piquancy to desserts. However, like double cream it is quite high in fat – 40% – so use it sparingly.

Fromage frais is a smooth, lightly tangy, lower fat to virtually fat-free 'cream' ideal for use in dressings, baked potatoes and desserts. Quark is a soft cheese made with skimmed milk and so is very low in fat. It is a traditional cheese for use in cheesecakes, but it is ideal for savoury dishes too. Cream and cottage cheeses are long time favourites, the latter being available in very low fat versions too for healthier eating.

Be sure to check all cheese labels first if you are looking for those made with vegetable rennet.

Dairy-free products

The unassuming soy bean is one of the best sources of high vegetable protein foods. As such, it is ideal as a base for dairy-free milks, creams, fat spreads, ice creams and cheeses, making it perfect for vegans and those with dairy product allergies. Use these products in the same way as their dairy counterparts, although those changing over will find that the soy products taste slightly sweeter.

Tofu, or bean curd, is made with soy milk and is particularly versatile in vegetarian cooking both as a main ingredient in recipes or to add a creamy and firm texture. On its own, tofu has little flavour, making it ideal to use as an absorber of other flavours, which is why it is so popular in Oriental cooking. Firm tofu/bean curd can be cut into cubes, marinated or smoked. It is very good fried in oil or grilled to a crisp, golden crust. A softer set tofu called silken tofu is a good substitute for cream in cooking and as such can be stirred into hot soups or used as a base for baked flans. Indeed at any time when cream or milk is called for in a recipe, tofu can be used. Not only high in protein, tofu is a good source of vitamins of the B group and iron, although as a vegetable source of iron, you will need to serve some vitamin C at the same meal to utilize it.

Mycoprotein (sold under the brand name Quorn), is a new man-made food which is a distant relation to the mushroom. Low in fat and calories it is high in protein with as much fibre as green vegetables. It cooks quickly, absorbing flavours as easily as soy bean curd and has a firmer texture. Good for stir-frying, stews and casseroles.

Nuts and seeds

Not only full of flavour, texture and colour, nuts and seeds are great nutritional power packs. But like cheese, they can be high in fats as well as proteins, so go easy.

Cheapest and most versatile are peanuts which are best bought unsalted or even better, roasted unsalted. Almonds (blanched or in flakes) are also very useful as are walnuts, pine nuts, hazelnuts and the more expensive cashews. Often it is nice to mix two or three together. But nuts can go rancid if stored too long (over six months or so), so if you are not a regular user, buy in small amounts. Unsalted pistachios are wonderful mixed with cooked rice or tossed into puddings (especially homemade ice creams).

For maximum flavour, lightly roast nuts first before chopping or crushing. Use them as crisp coatings too, but watch that they don't burn.

There is an increasing range of colourful and exciting seeds now in wholefood stores. Most useful are sunflower and sesame seeds, while pumpkin and melon seeds are most attractive scattered into salads or simply nibbled as a snack. Seeds for attractive garnish as well as flavour include poppy seeds, black mustard, fenugreek and caraway seeds. Most of all, nuts and seeds look simply stunning lined up in clean

storage jars on kitchen shelves, tempting you to toss them into a whole variety of dishes – hot and cold.

Herbs

Wherever possible, try to use fresh herbs. There are many that will grow easily and obligingly in pots and small back gardens as well as surviving the winter cold. Good candidates include shrubby rosemary, thyme, bay and sage. Even chives and marjoram can survive well into late autumn and return obligingly in early spring. However, more and more food shops are selling packs and bunches of fresh herbs which are grown commercially.

I find ethnic stores are great sources of good flavoured and cheap herbs. Most useful are flat leaf parsley, coriander, dill, basil, chives and mint. Do not just use one herb per dish either. Mix, match and experiment and use in generous amounts; although the more pungent such as tarragon, rosemary and sage, still need a cautious touch.

Handfuls of fresh leafy herbs are wonderful tossed into green salads making them very exciting – no need to chop them finely either. Pack a mug with washed sprigs then snip them roughly with scissors. Store leafy herbs loosely in polythene food bags in the fridge, spraying them lightly with water if they look limp. They spring back almost magically.

If you use dried herbs, then buy in small amounts and store in a dry, cool cupboard to retain their flavour. Replace dried herbs regularly as they soon lose their colour and flavour and end up tasting rather like dried grass.

Spices

The vegetarian's best friend! Warm, aromatic, colourful and easy to use, spices can lift the simplest dish into the supreme bracket. It is a misconception to think spices are pungently hot. Most are not; it is really only those of the chilli family — including cayenne – that are. Some spices are useful for both sweet and savoury dishes, such as nutmeg, cinnamon, mace, cloves, cardamom and ginger. Others, such as fenugreek, turmeric, paprika, cumin, coriander berries and chilli, are used for savoury dishes.

Spices are made for experimenting. Gradually you will learn which are the most pungent and to your liking. Some have glorious colours, like turmeric and paprika, others have a distinctive flavour. Add in cautious pinches at first until you decide what you enjoy most.

Spices are best roasted or fried first to bring out the aromatic oils. This can be done either in a hot oven or a frying pan. Where possible, use the seeds or grains of spices first and grind them down in a small electric spice mill or a pestle and mortar. Saffron (a most expensive spice) is best soaked briefly in a little warm water or milk to bring out its true flavour and pretty colour.

And don't restrict the use of spices to ethnic and exotic dishes. Add them to home cooked favourites – try macaroni cheese with paprika and cumin or fried eggs sprinkled with black mustard seeds.

SOUPS & STARTERS

Tantalising appetizers range from traditional favourites – including soups that could be served either before a main course or on their own as a light and wholesome meal – to more exotic dishes for elegant dinners.

Vegetable Stock

Use this versatile stock as the basis for all good soups and sauces. If you've an extra large saucepan, or preserving pan, why not make double the quantity and freeze several batches?

MAKES 2.25 LITRES/4 PINTS/10 CUPS
2 leeks, roughly chopped
3 sticks celery, roughly chopped
1 large onion, with skin, chopped
2 pieces fresh root ginger, chopped
3 garlic cloves, unpeeled
1 yellow pepper, seeded and chopped
1 parsnip, chopped
mushroom stalks
tomato peelings
45 ml/3 tbsp light soy sauce
3 bay leaves
bundle of parsley stalks
3 sprigs of fresh thyme
1 sprig of fresh rosemary
10 ml/2 tsp salt
ground black pepper
3.5 litres/6 pints/15 cups cold water

1 Put all the ingredients into a very large saucepan or a small preserving pan.

2 Bring slowly to the boil, then lower the heat and simmer for 30 minutes, stirring from time to time.

3 Allow the liquid and vegetables to cool. Strain, discard the vegetables and the stock is ready to use. Alternatively, chill or freeze the stock and keep it to use as required.

CRISP CROÛTONS

Easy to make and simple to store, these croûtons add a delightful touch to fresh homemade soups.

They are also an ideal way of using up stale bread. Speciality bread such as Ciabatta or baguettes can be thinly sliced to make the nicest, crunchiest croûtons, but everyday sliced loaves can be cut into interesting shapes for fun entertaining. Use a good quality, flavourless oil such as sunflower or groundnut, or for a fuller flavour brush with extra virgin olive oil. Alternatively, you could use a flavoured oil such as one with garlic and herbs or chilli.

Preheat the oven to 200°C/400°F/Gas 6. Place the croûtons on a baking sheet, brush with your chosen oil than bake for about 15 minutes until golden and crisp. They crisp up further as they cool. Store them in an airtight container for up to a week. Reheat in a warm oven if liked, before serving.

Sweetcorn and Potato Chowder

This hearty and substantial American soup is high in both fibre and flavour. It's wonderful served with thick crusty bread and topped with melted Cheddar cheese.

SERVES 4
1 onion, chopped
1 garlic clove, crushed
1 medium size potato, chopped
2 sticks celery, sliced
1 small green pepper, seeded, halved and sliced
30 ml/2 tbsp sunflower oil
25 g/1 oz/2 tbsp butter
600 ml/1 pint/2½ cups stock or water
salt and ground black pepper
300 ml/½ pint/1¼ cups milk
1 × 200 g/7 oz can butter beans
1 × 300 g/11 oz can sweetcorn kernels
good pinch dried sage

1 Put the onion, garlic, potato, celery and green pepper into a large saucepan with the oil and butter.

2 Heat the ingredients until sizzling then turn the heat down to low. Cover and sweat the vegetables gently for 10 minutes, shaking the pan occasionally.

3 Pour in the stock or water, season to taste and bring to the boil. Turn down the heat, cover and simmer gently for about 15 minutes.

4 Add the milk, beans and sweetcorn – including their liquors – and the sage. Simmer again for 5 minutes. Check the seasoning and serve hot.

All the Reds Soup 🌿

Vibrant in colour and taste, this soup is quickly made. Use a red onion – if you can find one – it will enhance the final appearance.

SERVES 4–6
1 red pepper, seeded and chopped
1 onion, chopped
1 garlic clove, crushed
30 ml/2 tbsp olive oil
1 × 400 g/14 oz can chopped tomatoes
1 litre/1¾ pints/4 cups stock
30 ml/2 tbsp long grain rice
30 ml/2 tbsp Worcestershire sauce
1 × 200 g/7 oz can red kidney beans
5 ml/1 tsp dried oregano
5 ml/1 tsp sugar
salt and ground black pepper
fresh parsley, chopped, and Cheddar
  cheese, grated, to garnish

1 Put the pepper, onion, garlic and oil into a large saucepan. Heat until sizzling then turn down to low. Cover and cook gently for 5 minutes.

2 Add the rest of the ingredients, except the garnishes, and bring to a boil. Stir well, then simmer – covered – for 15 minutes. Check the seasoning, garnish and serve hot. Omit the Cheddar cheese for a vegan soup.

Chinese Tofu and Lettuce Soup 🌿

This light, clear soup is brimming full of nourishing tasty pieces. Ideally, make this in a wok with the home-made vegetable stock.

SERVES 4
30 ml/2 tbsp groundnut or sunflower oil
200 g/7 oz smoked or marinated tofu,
  cubed
3 spring onions, sliced diagonally
2 garlic cloves, cut in thin strips
1 carrot, thinly sliced in rounds
1 litre/2 pints/5 cups stock
30 ml/2 tbsp soy sauce
15 ml/1 tbsp dry sherry or vermouth
5 ml/1 tsp sugar
115 g/4 oz Cos or Romaine lettuce,
  shredded
salt and ground black pepper

1 Heat the oil in a wok, then stir-fry the tofu cubes until browned. Drain and set aside on kitchen paper towel.

2 In the same oil, stir-fry the onions, garlic and carrot for 2 minutes. Pour in the stock, soy sauce and sherry or vermouth and sugar.

Spiced Indian Cauliflower Soup

Light and tasty, this creamy, mildly spicy soup is multi-purpose. It makes a wonderful warming first course, an appetizing quick meal and – when served chilled – is delicious for any summer menu.

SERVES 4–6
1 large potato, peeled and diced
1 small cauliflower, chopped
1 onion, chopped
15 ml/1 tbsp sunflower oil
1 garlic clove, crushed
15 ml/1 tbsp fresh ginger, grated
10 ml/2 tsp ground turmeric
5 ml/1 tsp cumin seeds
5 ml/1 tsp black mustard seeds
10 ml/2 tsp ground coriander
1 litre/1¾ pints/4 cups vegetable stock
300 ml/½ pint/1¼ cups natural yogurt
salt and ground black pepper
fresh coriander or parsley, to garnish

1 Put the potato, cauliflower and onion into a large saucepan with the oil and 45 ml/3 tbsp water. Heat until hot and bubbling, then cover and turn the heat down. Continue cooking the mixture for about 10 minutes.

2 Add the garlic, ginger and spices. Stir well and cook for another 2 minutes, stirring occasionally. Pour in the stock and season well. Bring to a boil, then cover and simmer for about 20 minutes. Stir in the yogurt, season well and garnish with coriander or parsley.

Winter Warmer Soup

Simmer a selection of popular winter root vegetables together for a warming and satisfying soup. Its creamy taste comes from adding crème frâiche just before serving.

SERVES 6
3 medium carrots, chopped
1 large potato, chopped
1 large parsnip, chopped
1 large turnip or small swede, chopped
1 onion, chopped
30 ml/2 tbsp sunflower oil
25 g/1 oz/2 tbsp butter
1.5 litres/2½ pints/6 cups water
salt and ground black pepper
1 piece fresh root ginger, peeled and grated
300 ml/½ pint/1¼ cups milk
45 ml/3 tbsp crème frâiche, fromage frais or natural yogurt
30 ml/2 tbsp fresh dill, chopped

1 Put the carrots, potato, parsnip, turnip or swede and onion into a large saucepan with the oil and butter. Fry lightly, then cover and sweat the vegetables on a very low heat for 15 minutes, shaking the pan occasionally.

2 Pour in the water, bring to a boil and season well. Cover and simmer for 20 minutes until the vegetables are soft.

3 Strain the vegetables, reserving the stock, add the ginger and purée in a food processor or blender until smooth.

4 Return the purée and stock to the pan. Add the milk and stir while the soup gently reheats.

5 Remove from the heat, stir in the crème frâiche, fromage frais or yogurt plus the dill, lemon juice and extra seasoning, if necessary. Reheat the soup, if you wish, but do not allow it to boil as you do so, or it may curdle.

Egg Flower Soup

For the very best flavour, you do need to use a homemade stock for this soup. The egg sets into pretty strands giving the soup a flowery look, hence the name.

SERVES 6
1 litre/1¾ pints/4 cups stock
45 ml/3 tbsp light soy sauce
30 ml/2 tbsp dry sherry or vermouth
3 spring onions, diagonally sliced
small piece fresh root ginger, shredded
4 large lettuce leaves, shredded
5 ml/1 tsp sesame seed oil
2 eggs, beaten
salt and ground black pepper
sesame seeds, to garnish

1 Pour the stock into a large saucepan. Add all the ingredients except the eggs and seeds. Bring to the boil and then cook for about 2 minutes.

2 Very carefully, pour the eggs in a thin, steady stream into the centre of the boiling liquid.

3 Count to three then quickly stir the soup. The egg will begin to cook and form long threads. Season to taste, ladle the soup into warm bowls and serve immediately sprinkled with sesame seeds.

Broccoli and Blue Brie Soup

A popular vegetable, broccoli makes a delicious soup with an appetizing deep green colour. For a tasty tang, stir in some cubes of blue Brie cheese just before serving.

SERVES 6
1 onion, chopped
450 g/1 lb broccoli spears, chopped
1 large courgette, chopped
1 large carrot, chopped
1 medium potato, chopped
25 g/1 oz/2 tbsp butter
30 ml/2 tbsp sunflower oil
2 litres/3½ pints/8 cups stock or water
about 75 g/3 oz blue Brie (or Dolcelatte) cheese, cubed
salt and ground black pepper
almond flakes, to garnish (optional)

VARIATION

Try using cauliflower instead of broccoli in this recipe. Stilton is a tasty alternative to Brie.

1 Put all the vegetables into a large saucepan, together with the butter and oil plus about 45 ml/3 tbsp stock or water.

2 Heat the ingredients until sizzling and stir well. Cover and cook gently for 15 minutes, shaking the pan occasionally, until all the vegetables soften.

3 Add the rest of the stock or water, season and bring to a boil, then cover and simmer gently for about 25–30 minutes.

4 Strain the vegetables and reserve the liquid. Purée the vegetables in a food processor or blender then return them to the pan with the reserved liquid.

5 Bring the soup back to a gentle boil and stir in the cheese until it melts. (Don't let the soup boil too hard or the cheese will become stringy.) Season to taste and garnish with a scattering of almond flakes.

Cream of Mushroom Soup

Homemade mushroom soup is quite, quite different from canned or packet soups. Add a few shiitake mushrooms (which are more readily available) to give your soup a richer flavour.

SERVES 4–6
450 g/1 lb open cup mushrooms, sliced
115 g/4 oz shiitake mushrooms, sliced
45 ml/3 tbsp sunflower oil
1 onion, chopped
1 stick celery, chopped
1.2 litres/2 pints/5 cups stock or water
30 ml/2 tbsp soy sauce
50 g/2 oz/¼ cup long grain rice
salt and ground black pepper
300 ml/½ pint/1¼ cups milk
fresh parsley, chopped, or almond flakes, to garnish

1 Put all the mushrooms into a large saucepan with the oil, onion and celery. Heat until sizzling, then cover and simmer for about 10 minutes, shaking the pan occasionally.

2 Add the stock or water, soy sauce, rice and seasoning. Bring to a boil then cover and simmer gently for 20 minutes until the vegetables and rice are soft.

3 Strain the vegetables, reserving the stock, and purée until smooth in a food processor or blender. Return the vegetables and reserved stock to the pan.

4 Stir in the milk, reheat until boiling and taste for seasoning. Serve hot sprinkled with a little chopped parsley and a few almond flakes.

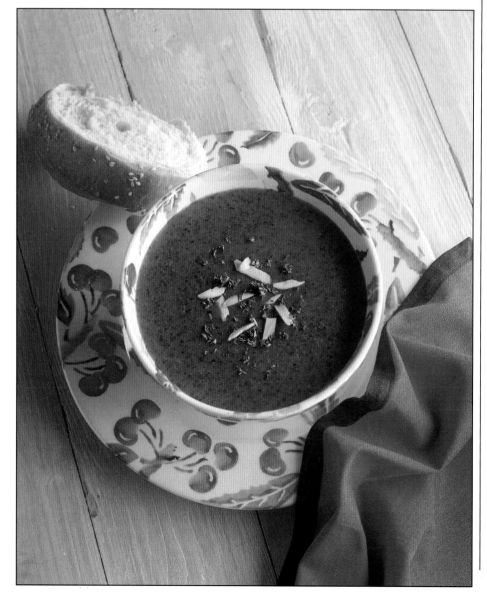

Classic Minestrone

This famous Italian soup has been much imitated around the world – with varying results. The homemade version is a delicious revelation and mouth-wateringly healthy with pasta, beans and fresh vegetables.

SERVES 4

1 large leek, thinly sliced
2 carrots, chopped
1 courgette, thinly sliced
115 g/4 oz whole green beans, halved
2 sticks celery, thinly sliced
45 ml/3 tbsp olive oil
1.5 litres/2½ pints/6¼ cups stock or water
1 × 400 g/14 oz can chopped tomatoes
15 ml/1 tbsp fresh basil, chopped
5 ml/1 tsp fresh thyme leaves, chopped
  or 2.5 ml/½ tsp dried thyme
salt and ground black pepper
1 × 400 g/14 oz can cannellini or kidney
  beans
50 g/2 oz/⅓ cup small pasta shapes or
  macaroni
fresh Parmesan cheese, finely grated, to
  garnish (optional)
fresh parsley, chopped, to garnish

1 Put all the fresh vegetables into a large saucepan with the olive oil. Heat until sizzling then cover, lower the heat and sweat the vegetables for 15 minutes, shaking the pan occasionally.

2 Add the stock or water, tomatoes, herbs and seasoning. Bring to the boil, replace the lid and simmer gently for about 30 minutes.

3 Add the beans and their liquor together with the pasta, and simmer for a further 10 minutes. Check the seasoning and serve hot sprinkled with the Parmesan cheese (if used) and parsley.

COOK'S TIP

Minestrone is also delicious served cold on a hot summer's day. In fact the flavour improves if made a day or two ahead and stored in the refrigerator. It can also be frozen and reheated.

Borscht

A simply stunning colour, this classic Russian soup is ideal to serve when you want to make something a little different. The flavour matures and improves too if it is made the day before it is needed.

SERVES 6
1 onion, chopped
450 g/1 lb raw beetroot, peeled and chopped
1 large cooking apple, chopped
2 celery sticks, chopped
½ red pepper, chopped
115 g/4 oz mushrooms, chopped
25 g/1 oz/2 tbsp butter
30 ml/2 tbsp sunflower oil
2 litres/3½ pints/8 cups stock or water
5 ml/1 tsp cumin seeds
pinch dried thyme
1 large bay leaf
fresh lemon juice
salt and ground black pepper
150 ml/¼ pint/⅔ cup soured cream
few sprigs fresh dill, to garnish

1 Place all the chopped vegetables into a large saucepan with the butter, oil and 45 ml/3 tbsp of the stock or water. Cover and cook gently for about 15 minutes, shaking the pan occasionally.

2 Stir in the cumin seeds and cook for a minute, then add the remaining stock or water, dried thyme, bay leaf, lemon juice and seasoning.

3 Bring to the boil, then cover and turn down to a gentle simmer. Cook for about 30 minutes.

4 Strain the vegetables and reserve the liquid. Pass the vegetables through a food processor or blender until they are smooth and creamy.

5 Return the vegetables to the pan, stir in the reserved stock and reheat. Check the seasoning.

6 Serve the borscht with swirls of soured cream and topped with a few sprigs of fresh dill.

VARIATION

This soup can be served fairly thick, as long as the vegetables are finely chopped first.

Beetroot is something of an under-valued vegetable, although popular in many European countries. For example, it is delicious served as a hot vegetable accompaniment with a creamy bechamel sauce and topped with crisp breadcrumbs. Alternatively, try it raw and coarsely grated, then tossed in dressing for a side salad.

Garlicky Mushrooms

Serve these on toast for a quick, tasty starter or pop them into small ramekins and serve with slices of warm crusty bread. Use some shitake mushrooms, if you can find them, for a richer flavour.

SERVES 4
450 g/1 lb button mushrooms, sliced if large
45 ml/3 tbsp olive oil
45 ml/3 tbsp stock or water
30 ml/2 tbsp dry sherry (optional)
3 garlic cloves, crushed
115 g/4 oz low fat soft cheese
30 ml/2 tbsp fresh parsley, chopped
15 ml/1 tbsp fresh chives, chopped
salt and ground black pepper

1 Put the mushrooms into a large saucepan with the olive oil, stock or water and sherry, if using. Heat until bubbling then cover and simmer for 5 minutes.

2 Add the garlic and stir well. Cook for a further 2 minutes. Remove the mushrooms with a slotted spoon and set them aside. Cook the liquor until it reduces down to 30 ml/2 tbsp. Remove from the heat and stir in the cheese and herbs.

3 Stir the mixture well until the cheese melts then return the mushrooms to the pan so that they become coated with the cheesy mixture. Season to taste.

4 Pile the mushrooms onto thick slabs of hot toast. Alternatively, spoon them into four ramekins and serve accompanied by slices of crusty bread.

Ricotta and Borlotti Bean Pâté

A lovely light yet full-flavoured pâté. For an attractive presentation, spoon the pâté into small, oiled ring moulds, turn out and fill with some whole borlotti beans, simply dressed with lemon juice, olive oil and fresh herbs.

SERVES 4
1 × 400 g/14 oz can borlotti beans, drained
1 garlic clove, crushed
175 g/6 oz ricotta cheese (or other cream cheese)
50 g/2 oz/4 tbsp butter, melted
juice of ½ lemon
salt and ground black pepper
30 ml/2 tbsp fresh parsley, chopped
15 ml/1 tbsp fresh thyme or dill, chopped
TO SERVE
extra canned beans (optional)
fresh lemon juice, olive oil and chopped herbs (optional)
salad leaves, radish slices and few sprigs fresh dill, to garnish

1 Blend the beans, garlic, cheese, butter, lemon juice and seasoning in a food processor until smooth.

2 Add the chopped herbs and continue to blend. Spoon into one serving dish or four lightly oiled ramekins, the bases lined with discs of non-stick baking paper. Chill the pâté so that it sets firm.

3 If serving with extra beans, dress them with lemon juice, olive oil and herbs, season well and spoon on top. Garnish with salad leaves and serve with warm crusty bread or toast.

4 If serving individually, turn each pâté out of its ramekin onto a small plate and remove the disc of paper. Top with radish slices and sprigs of dill.

VARIATION

You could try other canned pulses for this recipe, although the softer lentils would not be suitable. Butter (lima) beans are surprisingly good. For an attractive presentation fill the centre with dark red kidney beans and chopped fresh green beans.

Mediterranean Vegetables with Tahini

Wonderfully colourful, this starter is easily prepared in advance. For an *al fresco* meal, why not grill the vegetables on a barbecue? Tahini is a paste made from sesame seeds.

SERVES 4

2 peppers, red, green or yellow, seeded and quartered
2 courgettes, halved lengthways
2 small aubergines, degorged and halved lengthways
1 fennel bulb, quartered
olive oil
salt and ground black pepper
115 g/4 oz Greek Halloumi cheese, sliced

TAHINI CREAM

225 g/8 oz/1 cup tahini paste
1 garlic cloves, crushed
30 ml/2 tbsp olive oil
30 ml/2 tbsp fresh lemon juice
120 ml/4 fl oz/½ cup cold water

1 Preheat the grill or barbecue until hot. Brush the vegetables with the oil and grill until just browned, turning once. (If the peppers blacken, don't worry. The skins can be peeled off.) Cook the vegetables until just softened.

2 Place the vegetables in a shallow dish and season. Allow to cool. Meanwhile, brush the cheese slices with oil and grill these on both sides until just charred. Remove them with a palette knife.

3 To make the tahini cream, place all the ingredients, except the water, in a food processor or blender. Whizz for a few seconds to mix, then, with the motor still running, pour in the water and blend until smooth.

4 Serve the vegetables and cheese on a platter and trickle over the cream. Delicious served with warm pitta or naan breads.

Imam Bayildi

Legend has it that a Muslim holy man – the Imam – was so overwhelmed by this dish that he fainted in sheer delight! Translated, Imam Bayildi means 'The Imam fainted'.

SERVES 4

2 medium aubergines, degorged (see Cook's Tip) and halved lengthways
salt
60 ml/4 tbsp olive oil
2 large onions, sliced thinly
2 garlic cloves, crushed
1 green pepper, seeded and sliced
1 × 400 g/14 oz can chopped tomatoes
30 g/1½ oz sugar
5 ml/1 tsp ground coriander
ground black pepper
30 ml/2 tbsp fresh coriander or parsley, chopped

1 Using a sharp knife, slash the flesh of the aubergines a few times. Sprinkle with salt and place in a colander for about half an hour. Rinse well and pat dry.

2 Gently fry the aubergines, cut side down, in the oil for 5 minutes, then drain and place in a shallow ovenproof dish.

3 In the same pan gently fry the onions, garlic and green pepper, adding extra oil if necessary. Cook for about 10 minutes, until the vegetables have softened.

4 Add the tomatoes, sugar, ground coriander and seasoning and cook for about 5 minutes until the mixture is reduced. Stir in the chopped coriander or parsley.

5 Spoon this mixture on top of the aubergines. Preheat the oven to 190° C/ 375° F/Gas 5, cover and bake for about 30–35 minutes. When cooked, cool, then chill. Serve cold with crusty bread.

COOK'S TIP

To degorge aubergines: sprinkle cut slices with salt and allow the juices that form to drain away in a colander. After 30 minutes or so, rinse well and pat dry. Degorged aubergines are less bitter and easier to cook.

Twice-baked Goats' Cheese Soufflés

A good chef's trick is to reheat small baked soufflés out of their ramekins to serve with a salad. They puff up again and the outsides become nice and crispy. If you prefer, you can substitute another full-flavoured cheese such as Cheddar or Parmesan.

SERVES 6
25 g/1 oz/2 tbsp butter
25 g/1 oz/3 tbsp plain flour
300 ml/½ pint/1¼ cups hot milk
pinch cayenne pepper
squeeze of lemon juice
salt and ground black pepper
100 g/3½ oz semi-hard goats' cheese, crumbled
2 eggs, separated
melted butter, for brushing
25 g/1 oz/3 tbsp dried breadcrumbs
25 g/1 oz/3 tbsp ground hazelnuts or walnuts
2 egg whites
salad garnish (optional)

1 Melt the butter and stir in the flour. Cook to a roux for a minute then gradually whisk in the hot milk to make a thick white sauce.

VARIATION

There is another good chef's trick – making soufflés in advance and chilling them unbaked. It helps to add an extra egg white or two when whisking, depending on the mixture. It is also possible to freeze unbaked soufflés in small ramekins and then to bake them from frozen, allowing an extra 5 or 10 minutes' baking time.

2 Simmer for a minute then season with cayenne, lemon juice, salt and pepper. Remove the pan from the heat and stir in the cheese until it melts. Cool slightly then beat in the egg yolks.

3 Brush the insides of six ramekins with the melted butter and coat them with the breadcrumbs and nuts mixed together. Shake out any excess.

4 Preheat the oven to 190°C/375°F/ Gas 5 and prepare a bain marie – a roasting pan with boiling water.

5 Whisk the four egg whites to the soft peak stage and carefully fold them into the main mixture using a figure of eight motion. Spoon into the ramekins.

6 Place the soufflés in the bain marie and bake for about 12–15 minutes until risen and golden brown. You can of course serve them at this stage; otherwise allow to cool then chill.

7 To serve twice-baked, reheat the oven to the same temperature. Run a knife round the inside of each ramekin and turn out each soufflé onto a baking tray.

8 Bake the soufflés for about 12 minutes. Serve on prepared plates with a dressed salad garnish.

Tricolour Salad

This can be a simple starter if served on individual salad plates, or part of a light buffet meal laid out on a platter. When lightly salted, tomatoes make their own flavoursome dressing with their natural juices.

SERVES 4–6
1 small red onion, sliced thinly
6 large full-flavoured tomatoes
extra virgin olive oil, to sprinkle
50 g/2 oz/small bunch rocket or
  watercress, roughly chopped
salt and ground black pepper
175 g/6 oz Mozzarella cheese, thinly sliced
  or grated
30 ml/2 tbsp pine nuts (optional)

1 Soak the onion slices in a bowl of cold water for 30 minutes, then drain and pat dry. Skin the tomatoes by slashing and dipping briefly in boiling water. Remove the core and slice the flesh.

2 Slice the tomatoes and arrange half on a large platter, or divide them between small plates.

3 Sprinkle liberally with olive oil then layer with the chopped rocket or cress, and soaked onion slices, seasoning well. Add in the cheese, sprinkling over more oil and seasoning as you go.

4 Repeat with the remaining tomato slices, salad leaves, cheese and oil.

5 Season well to finish and complete with some oil and a good scattering of pine nuts. Cover the salad and chill for at least 2 hours before serving.

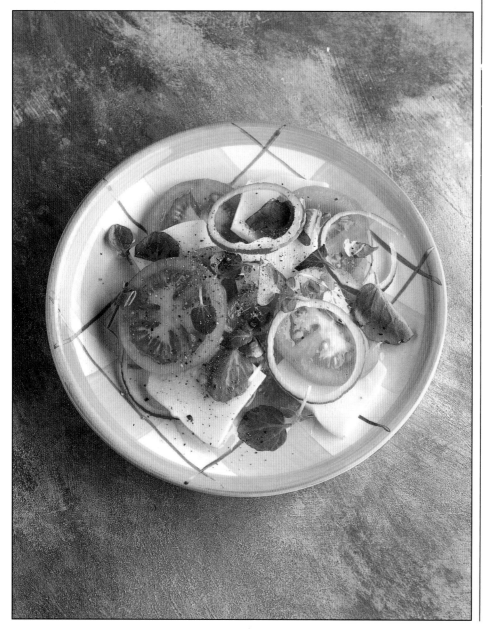

Guacamole Salsa in Red Leaves

This lovely, light summery starter looks so attractive arranged in cups of radicchio leaves. Serve with chunks of warm garlic bread.

SERVES 4
2 tomatoes, skinned and chopped
15 ml/1 tbsp grated onion
1 garlic clove, crushed
1 green chilli, halved, seeded and chopped
2 ripe avocadoes
30 ml/2 tbsp olive oil
2.5 ml/½ tsp ground cumin
30 ml/2 tbsp fresh coriander or parsley, chopped
juice of 1 lime
salt and ground black pepper
leaves from radicchio lettuce

1 Using a sharp knife, slash a small cross on the top of the tomatoes, then dip them briefly in a bowl of boiling water. The skins will slip off easily. Remove the core and chop the flesh.

2 Put the tomato flesh into a bowl together with the onion, garlic and chopped chilli. Halve the avocadoes, remove the stones then scoop the flesh into the bowl, mashing it with a fork.

3 Add the remaining ingredients, except for the radicchio leaves, and mix well together, seasoning to taste.

4 Lay the radicchio leaves on a platter and spoon in the salsa. Serve immediately as avocadoes go black when exposed to the air.

COOK'S TIP

Take care when cutting chillies. The juice can sting, so be careful not to rub your eyes until you have washed your hands.

Stuffed Artichokes

Globe artichokes are a little fiddly to prepare but their delicious taste makes it all worthwhile, especially when stuffed with nuts, mushrooms and sun-dried tomatoes. This dish can be prepared in advance and reheated before serving.

SERVES 4
4 medium globe artichokes
salt
lemon slices
STUFFING
1 medium onion, chopped
1 garlic clove, crushed
45 ml/3 tbsp olive oil
115 g/4 oz mushrooms, chopped
1 medium carrot, grated
40 g/1½ oz sun-dried tomatoes in oil,
    drained and sliced
leaves from a sprig of thyme
about 45–60 ml/3–4 tbsp water
ground black pepper
115 g/4 oz/2 cups fresh breadcrumbs
extra olive oil, to cook
fresh parsley, chopped, to garnish

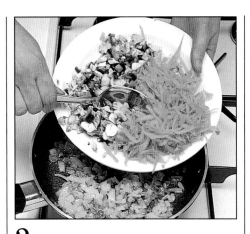

2 To make the stuffing for the artichokes, gently fry the onion and garlic in the oil for 5 minutes, then add the mushrooms, carrot, sun-dried tomatoes and thyme.

3 Stir in the water, season well and cook for a further 5 minutes, then mix in the breadcrumbs.

VARIATION

For a lighter meal, rather than stuff the artichokes, you could simply fill the centres with home-made mayonnaise or serve with a dish of vinaigrette or melted butter for dipping the leaves.

4 Pull the artichoke leaves apart and pull out the purple-tipped central leaves. Using a small teaspoon, scrape out the hairy choke, making sure that you remove it all. Discard it.

5 Spoon the stuffing into the centre of the artichoke, and push the leaves back into shape. Put the artichokes into an ovenproof dish and pour a little oil into the centre of each one.

6 Half an hour before serving, heat the oven to 190°C/375°F/Gas 5 and bake the artichokes for about 20–25 minutes until heated through. Serve garnished with a little chopped fresh parsley on top.

1 Boil the artichokes in plenty of salted water with a few slices of lemon for about 30 minutes, or until a leaf pulls easily from the base. Strain through a colander and cool the artichokes, laying them upside down.

Bruschetta with Goats' Cheese and Tapenade

Simple to prepare in advance, this appetizing dish can be served as a starter or at finger buffets. Make sure that you finely chop the ingredients for the tapenade.

SERVES 4–6
TAPENADE
1 × 400 g/14 oz can black olives, stoned and finely chopped
50 g/2 oz sun-dried tomatoes in oil, chopped
30 ml/2 tbsp capers, chopped
15 ml/1 tbsp green peppercorns, in brine, crushed
45–60 ml/3–4 tbsp olive oil
2 garlic cloves, crushed
45 ml/3 tbsp fresh basil, chopped, or 5 ml/1 tsp dried basil
salt and ground black pepper
BASES
12 slices Ciabatta or other crusty bread
olive oil, for brushing
2 garlic cloves, halved
115 g/4 oz soft goats' cheese (or plain cream cheese)
fresh herb sprigs, to garnish

1 Mix the tapenade ingredients all together and check the seasoning. It should not need too much. Allow to marinate overnight, if possible.

2 To make the bruschetta, grill both sides of the bread lightly until golden. Brush one side with oil and then rub with a cut clove of garlic. Set aside until ready to serve.

3 Spread the bruschetta with the cheese, roughing it up with a fork, and spoon the tapenade on top. Garnish with sprigs of herbs.

COOK'S TIP

The bruschetta is nicest grilled over a open barbecue flame, if possible. Failing that a grill will do, but avoid using a toaster – it gives too even a colour and the bruschetta is supposed to look quite rustic.

Warm Avocadoes with Tangy Topping

Lightly grilled with a tasty topping of red onions and cheese, this dish makes a delightful alternative to the rather humdrum avocado vinaigrette.

SERVES 4
1 small red onion, sliced
1 garlic clove, crushed
15 ml/1 tbsp sunflower oil
Worcestershire sauce
2 ripe avocadoes, halved and stoned
2 small tomatoes, sliced
15 ml/1 tbsp fresh chopped basil, marjoram or parsley
50 g/2 oz Lancashire or Mozzarella cheese, sliced
salt and ground black pepper

1 Gently fry the onion and garlic in the oil for about 5 minutes until just softened. Shake in a little Worcestershire sauce.

2 Preheat a grill. Place the avocado halves on the grill pan and spoon the onions into the centre.

3 Divide the tomato slices and fresh herbs between the four halves and top each one with the cheese.

4 Season well and grill until the cheese melts and starts to brown.

VARIATION

Avocadoes are wonderful served in other hot dishes too. Try them chopped and tossed into hot pasta or sliced and layered in a lasagne.

Tempura Vegetables with Dipping Sauce

A Japanese favourite, these are thinly sliced, fresh vegetables fried in a light crispy batter and served with a small bowl of flavoured soy sauce. For the best results, serve these immediately so the batter remains crisp. Tempura also makes a delicious party piece.

SERVES 4–6
1 medium courgette, sliced in thin sticks
1 red pepper, seeded and cut in wedges
3 large mushrooms, quartered
1 fennel bulb, cut in wedges with root attached
½ medium aubergine, thinly sliced
oil, for deep frying
SAUCE
45 ml/3 tbsp soy sauce
15 ml/1 tbsp medium dry sherry
5 ml/1 tsp sesame seed oil
few shreds fresh ginger or spring onion
BATTER
1 egg
115 g/4 oz/1 cup plain flour
175 ml/6 fl oz/¾ cup cold water
salt and ground black pepper

1 Prepare all the vegetables and lay them out on a tray, together with sheets of kitchen paper towel for draining the vegetables after cooking.

2 Mix the sauce ingredients together by whisking them in a jug or shaking them together in a sealed jar. Pour into a bowl.

3 Half fill a deep frying pan with oil and preheat to a temperature of about 190°C/375°F. Quickly whisk the batter ingredients together but don't overbeat them. It doesn't matter if the batter is a little lumpy.

4 Fry the vegetables in stages by dipping a few quickly into the batter and lowering into the hot oil in a wire basket. Fry for just a minute until golden brown and crisp. Drain on the paper towel.

5 Repeat until all the vegetables are fried. Keep those you have cooked, uncovered, in a warm oven while you fry the rest. Serve the vegetables on a large platter alongside the dipping sauce.

COOK'S TIP

Successful deep frying can be quite tricky and a bit hazardous. First, never leave the pan of oil unattended while the heat is turned on. If you have to leave the stove, then turn the oil off. The oil will drop in temperature during cooking so keep re-heating it between batches.

Sweetcorn Blinis with Dill Cream

A mouth-watering and unusual starter, these blinis are also suitable for a cocktail buffet. Ideally make them an hour or two before you serve them, although the batter will stand for longer.

SERVES 6–8

75 g/3 oz/¾ cup plain flour
75 g/3 oz/⅔ cup wholemeal flour
250 ml/8 fl oz/1 cup buttermilk
4 small eggs, beaten
2.5 ml/½ tsp salt
2.5 ml/½ tsp baking powder
25 g/1 oz/2 tbsp butter, melted
good pinch bicarbonate of soda
15 ml/1 tbsp hot water
1 × 200 g/7 oz can sweetcorn kernels, drained
oil, for the griddle

DILL CREAM
200 g/7 oz crème fraîche
30 ml/2 tbsp fresh dill, chopped
30 ml/2 tbsp fresh chives, chopped
salt and ground black pepper

1 Mix the two flours and buttermilk together until completely smooth. Cover and leave to chill for about 8 hours in the refrigerator.

2 Beat in the eggs, salt, baking powder and butter. Mix the bicarbonate with the hot water and add this too, along with the sweetcorn kernels.

3 Heat a griddle or heavy based frying pan until quite hot. Brush with a little oil and drop spoonfuls of the blinis mixture on to it. The mixture should start to sizzle immediately.

4 Cook until holes appear on the top and the mixture looks almost set. Using a palette knife flip the blinis over and cook briefly. Stack the blinis under a clean tea towel while you make the rest.

5 To make the cream, simply blend the crème fraîche with the herbs and seasoning. Serve the blinis with a few spoonfuls of cream and garnished with sliced radishes and herbs.

LIGHT LUNCHES & SUPPERS

For tempting lunches that are not too filling and tasty television suppers, experiment with these glorious recipes, from those that include protein-rich ingredients such as tofu to irresistible cheese and pasta dishes.

Mexican Brunch Eggs

Instead of eggs on toast, why not try them on fried corn tortillas with chillies and creamy avocado? Canned tortillas are readily available from larger supermarkets or delicatessens.

SERVES 4
oil, for frying
8 tortilla corn pancakes
1 avocado
1 large tomato
50 g/2 oz/4 tbsp butter
8 eggs
4 jalepeno chillies, sliced
salt and ground black pepper
15 ml/1 tbsp fresh coriander, chopped,
   to garnish

1 Heat the oil and fry the tortillas for a few seconds each side. Remove and drain. Keep the tortillas warm.

2 Halve, stone and peel the avocado, then cut into slices. Dip the tomato into boiling water, then skin and chop roughly.

3 Melt the butter in a frying pan and fry the eggs, in batches, sunny side up.

4 Place two tortillas on four plates, slip an egg on each and top with sliced chillies, avocado and tomato. Season and serve garnished with fresh coriander.

Fried Tomatoes with Polenta Crust

If you saw the film 'Fried Green Tomatoes' then you should enjoy this dish! No need to search for home-grown green tomatoes – any slightly under-ripe ones will do.

SERVES 4
4 large firm under-ripe tomatoes
115 g/4 oz/1 cup polenta or coarse
   cornmeal
5 ml//1 tsp dried oregano
2.5 ml/½ tsp garlic powder
plain flour, for dredging
1 egg, beaten with seasoning
oil, for deep fat frying

1 Cut the tomatoes into thick slices. Mix the polenta or cornmeal with the oregano and garlic powder.

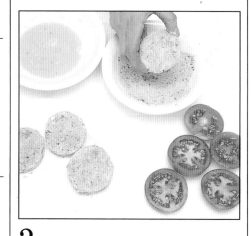

2 Put the flour, egg and polenta into different bowls. Dip the tomato slices into the flour, then into the egg and finally into the polenta.

3 Fill a shallow frying pan a third full of oil and heat steadily until quite hot.

4 Slip the tomato slices into the oil carefully, a few at a time, and fry on each side until crisp. Remove and drain. Repeat with the remaining tomatoes, reheating the oil in between. Serve with salad.

Mushroom and Chilli Carbonara

For a richer mushroom flavour, use a small pack of dried Italian porcini mushrooms in this quick eggy sauce, and for an extra spicy zing, toss in some chilli flakes too.

SERVES 4

1 × 15 g/½ oz pack dried porcini
    mushrooms
300 ml/½ pint/1¼ cups hot water
225 g/8 oz spaghetti
1 garlic clove, crushed
25 g/1 oz/2 tbsp butter
15 ml/1 tbsp olive oil
225 g/8 oz button or chestnut
    mushrooms, sliced
5 ml/1 tsp dried chilli flakes
2 eggs
300 ml/½ pint/1¼ cups single cream
salt and ground black pepper
fresh Parmesan cheese, grated, and
    parsley, chopped, to serve

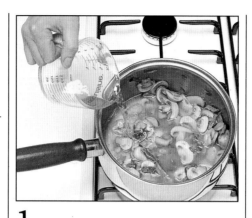

1 Soak the dried mushrooms in the hot water for 15 minutes, drain and reserve the liquor.

2 Boil the spaghetti according to the instructions on the packet in salted water. Drain and rinse in cold water.

3 In a large saucepan, lightly sauté the garlic with the butter and oil for half a minute then add the mushrooms, including the soaked porcini ones, and the dried chilli flakes, and stir well. Cook for about 2 minutes, stirring a few times.

4 Pour in the reserved mushroom stock and boil to reduce slightly.

5 Beat the eggs with the cream and season well. Return the cooked spaghetti to the pan and toss in the eggs and cream. Reheat, without boiling, and serve hot sprinkled with Parmesan cheese and chopped parsley.

VARIATION

Instead of mushrooms, try using either finely sliced and sautéed leeks or perhaps coarsely shredded lettuce with peas. If chilli flakes are too hot and spicy for you, then try the delicious alternative of skinned and chopped tomatoes with torn, fresh basil leaves.

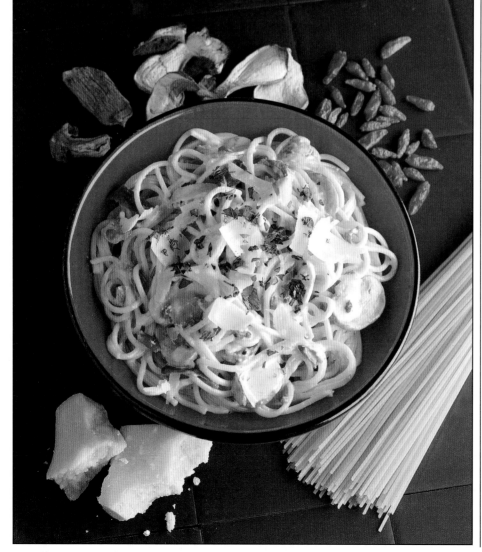

Tagliatelle with 'Hit-the-pan' Salsa

It is possible to make a hot filling meal within just fifteen minutes with this quick-cook salsa sauce. If you don't have time to peel the tomatoes, then don't bother.

SERVES 2
115 g/4 oz tagliatelle
45 ml/3 tbsp olive oil, preferably extra virgin
3 large tomatoes
1 garlic clove, crushed
4 spring onions, sliced
1 green chilli, halved, seeded and sliced
juice of 1 orange (optional)
30 ml/2 tbsp fresh parsley, chopped
salt and ground black pepper
cheese, grated, to garnish (optional)

1 Boil the tagliatelle in plenty of salted water until it is *al dente*. Drain and toss in a little of the oil. Season well.

2 Skin the tomatoes by dipping them briefly in a bowl of boiling water. The skins should slip off easily. Chop the tomatoes roughly.

3 Heat the remaining oil until it is quite hot and stir-fry the garlic, onions and chilli for a minute. The pan should sizzle.

4 Add the tomatoes, orange juice (if using) and parsley. Season well and stir in the tagliatelle to reheat. Serve with the grated cheese (if used).

COOK'S TIP

You could use any pasta shape for this recipe. It would be particularly good with large rigatoni or linguini, or as a sauce for fresh ravioli or tortellini.

Cheesy Bubble and Squeak

This London breakfast dish is enjoying something of a revival. Originally made on Mondays with leftover potatoes and cabbage from the Sunday lunch, it is suitable for any light meal occasion. For breakfast, serve the bubble and squeak with eggs, grilled tomatoes and mushrooms.

SERVES 4

about 450 g/1 lb/3 cups mashed potato
about 225 g/8 oz cooked cabbage or kale, shredded
1 egg, beaten
115 g/4 oz Cheddar cheese, grated
fresh nutmeg, grated
salt and ground black pepper
plain flour, for coating
oil, for frying

1 Mix the potatoes with the cabbage or kale, egg, cheese, nutmeg and seasoning. Divide and shape into eight patties.

2 Chill for an hour or so, if possible, as this enables the mixture to become firm and makes it easier to fry. Toss the patties in the flour. Heat about 1 cm/½ in of oil in a frying pan until it is quite hot.

3 Carefully slide the patties into the oil and fry on each side for about 3 minutes until golden and crisp. Drain on kitchen paper towel and serve hot and crisp.

Cheese and Chutney Toasties

Quick cheese on toast can be made quite memorable with a few tasty additions. Serve these scrumptious toasties with a simple salad.

SERVES 4

4 slices wholemeal bread, thickly sliced
butter or low fat spread
115 g/4 oz Cheddar cheese, grated
5 ml/1 tsp dried thyme
ground black pepper
30 ml/2 tbsp chutney or relish

1 Toast the bread slices lightly on each side then spread sparingly with butter or low fat spread.

2 Mix the cheese and thyme together and season with pepper.

3 Spread the chutney or relish on the toast and divide the cheese between the four slices.

4 Return to the grill and cook until browned and bubbling. Cut into halves, diagonally, and serve with salad.

Risotto Primavera

Real Italian risottos should be creamy and full of flavour. They are best made freshly and do need frequent stirring, but this can be done in between other jobs in the kitchen. For best results use a quality Arborio rice which has a good *al dente* bite.

SERVES 4

1 litre/1¾ pints/4 cups hot stock, preferably homemade
1 red onion, chopped
2 garlic cloves, crushed
30 ml/2 tbsp olive oil
25 g/1 oz/2 tbsp butter
225 g/8 oz/1¼ cups risotto rice (do not rinse)
45 ml/3 tbsp dry white wine
115 g/4 oz asparagus spears or green beans, sliced and blanched
2 young carrots, sliced and blanched
50 g/2 oz baby button mushrooms
salt and ground black pepper
50 g/2 oz Pecorino or Parmesan cheese, grated

1 It is important to follow the steps for making real risotto so that you achieve the right texture. First, heat the stock in a saucepan to simmering.

2 Next to it, in a large saucepan, sauté the onion and garlic in the oil and butter for 3 minutes.

3 Stir in the rice making sure each grain is coated well in the oil, then stir in the wine. Allow to reduce down and spoon in two ladles of hot stock, stirring continuously.

4 Allow this to bubble down then add more stock and stir again. Continue like this, ladling in the stock and stirring frequently for up to 20 minutes, by which time the rice will have swelled greatly.

5 Mix in the asparagus or beans, carrots and mushrooms, seasoning well, and cook for a minute or two more. Serve immediately in bowls with a scattering of grated cheese.

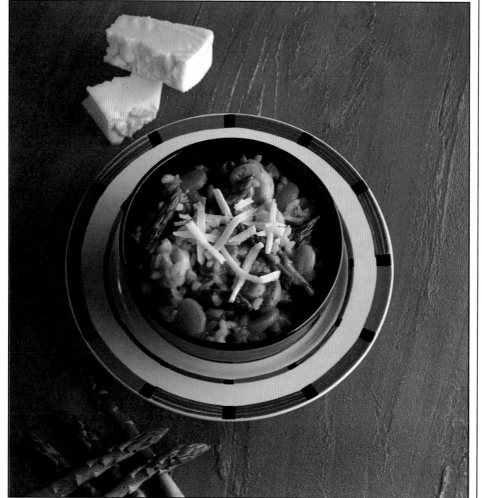

VARIATION

If you have any left-over risotto, shape it into small balls and then coat in beaten egg and dried breadcrumbs. Chill for 30 minutes before deep frying in hot oil until golden and crisp.

Kitchiri

This is the Indian original which inspired the classic breakfast dish known as kedgeree. Made with basmati rice and small tasty lentils this will make an ample supper or brunch dish.

SERVES 4

115 g/4 oz/1 cup Indian masoor
   dhal or Continental green lentils
1 onion, chopped
1 garlic clove, crushed
50 g/2 oz/4 tbsp vegetarian ghee or butter
30 ml/2 tbsp sunflower oil
225 g/8 oz/1¼ cups easy-cook basmati rice
10 ml/2 tsp ground coriander
10 ml/2 tsp cumin seeds
2 cloves
3 cardamom pods
2 bay leaves
1 stick cinnamon
1 litre/1¾ pints/4 cups stock
30 ml/2 tbsp tomato purée
salt and ground black pepper
45 ml/3 tbsp fresh coriander or parsley,
   chopped

1 Cover the dhal or lentils with boiling water and soak for 30 minutes. Drain and boil in fresh water for 10 minutes. Drain once more and set aside.

2 Fry the onion and garlic in the ghee or butter and oil in a large saucepan for about 5 minutes.

3 Add the rice, stir well to coat the grains in the ghee or butter and oil, then stir in the spices. Cook gently for a minute or so.

4 Add the lentils, stock, tomato purée and seasoning. Bring to the boil, then cover and simmer for 20 minutes until the stock is absorbed and the lentils and rice are just soft. Stir in the coriander or parsley and check the seasoning. Remove the cinnamon stick and bay leaf.

Pissaladière

A French Mediterranean classic, this is a delicious and colourful tart full of punchy flavour. Ideally, put the base and fillings together just when serving so the base remains crisp.

SERVES 6
PASTRY
225 g/8 oz/2 cups plain flour
115 g/4 oz/8 tbsp butter or sunflower margarine
5 ml/1 tsp dried mixed herbs
pinch salt
FILLING
2 large onions, thinly sliced
2 garlic cloves, crushed
45 ml/3 tbsp olive oil
fresh nutmeg, grated, to taste
1 × 400 g/14 oz can chopped tomatoes
5 ml/1 tsp sugar
leaves from small sprig of thyme
salt and ground black pepper
75 g/3 oz/⅔ cup stoned black olives, sliced
30 ml/2 tbsp capers
fresh parsley, chopped, to garnish

1 Rub the flour and butter or margarine together until it forms fine crumbs, then mix in the herbs and salt. Mix to a firm dough with cold water. Preheat the oven to 190°C/375°F/Gas 5.

2 Roll out and line a 21 cm/9 in flan dish and bake blind, removing the baking beans and paper for the last 5 minutes for the pastry to crisp up. Cool.

3 Gently fry the onions and garlic in the oil for about 10 minutes until quite soft and mix in the nutmeg.

4 Stir in the tomatoes, sugar, thyme and seasoning and simmer gently for about 10 minutes until the mixture is reduced and slightly syrupy.

5 Remove from the heat and allow to cool. Mix in the olives and capers.

6 When ready to serve, spoon into the flan case, sprinkle with some fresh chopped parsley and serve at room temperature.

VARIATION

To serve Pissaladière hot, top with grated cheese and grill until the cheese is golden and bubbling. The crisp-baked pastry case can be used as a base for a number of other vegetable mixtures. Try filling it with a Russian Salad – chopped, cooked root vegetables, including potato and carrot, mixed with peas, beans and onions, blended with mayonnaise and soured cream. Top with slices of hard-boiled egg and garnish with chopped fresh herbs.

Multi Mushroom Stroganoff

A pan fry of sliced mushrooms swirled with soured cream is made especially interesting if two or three varieties of mushroom are used. It is even more delicious if you can incorporate woodland or wild mushrooms.

SERVES 3–4
45 ml/3 tbsp olive oil
450 g/1 lb edible mushrooms (including ceps, shiitakes or oysters), sliced
3 spring onions, sliced
2 garlic cloves, crushed
30 ml/2 tbsp dry sherry or vermouth
salt and ground black pepper
300 ml/½ pint/1¼ cups soured cream or crème fraîche
15 ml/1 tbsp fresh marjoram or thyme leaves, chopped
fresh parsley, chopped

1 Heat the oil in a large frying pan and fry the mushrooms gently, stirring them occasionally until they are softened and just cooked.

2 Add the spring onions, garlic and sherry or vermouth and cook for a minute more. Season well.

3 Stir in the soured cream or crème fraîche and heat to just below boiling. Stir in the marjoram or thyme then scatter over the parsley. Serve with rice, pasta or boiled new potatoes.

Butter Bean and Pesto Pasta

Buy good quality, ready-made pesto, rather than making your own. Pesto forms the basis of several very tasty sauces, and it is especially good with butter beans.

SERVES 4
225 g/8 oz pasta shapes
salt and ground black pepper
fresh nutmeg, grated
30 ml/2 tbsp extra virgin olive oil
1 × 400 g/14 oz can butter beans, drained
45 ml/3 tbsp pesto sauce
150 ml/¼ pint/⅔ cup single cream
TO SERVE
45 ml/3 tbsp pine nuts
cheese, grated (optional)
sprigs of fresh basil, to garnish (optional)

1 Boil the pasta until *al dente*, then drain, leaving it a little wet. Return the pasta to the pan, season, and stir in the nutmeg and oil.

2 Heat the beans in a saucepan with the pesto and cream, stirring it until it begins to simmer. Toss the beans and pesto into the pasta and mix well.

3 Serve in bowls topped with pine nuts, and add a little grated cheese and basil sprigs if you wish.

Baked Potatoes and Three Fillings

Potatoes baked in their jackets and packed with a variety of fillings make an excellent and nourishing meal. Although they have been cooked here in a conventional oven, potatoes can be baked more quickly and just as successfully in a microwave.

4 medium size baking potatoes
olive oil, for greasing
sea salt, to serve

1 Preheat the oven to 200°C/400°F/ Gas 6. Score the potatoes with a cross and rub all over with the olive oil.

2 Place on a baking sheet and cook for 45–60 minutes until a knife inserted into the centres indicates they are cooked.

3 Cut the potatoes open along the score lines and push up the flesh from the base with your fingers. Season with salt and fill with your chosen filling.

EACH FILLING IS FOR FOUR POTATOES

RED BEAN FILLING
1 × 425 g/15 oz can red kidney beans
200 g/7 oz low fat cheese or cream cheese
30 ml/2 tbsp mild chilli sauce
5 ml/1 tsp ground cumin

Red Bean – drain the beans, heat in a pan or microwave and stir in the cream cheese, chilli sauce and cumin.

SOY VEGETABLES FILLING
2 leeks, thinly sliced
2 carrots, cut in sticks
1 courgette, thinly sliced
115 g/4 oz baby sweetcorn, halved
45 ml/3 tbsp groundnut or sunflower oil
115 g/4 oz button mushrooms, sliced
45 ml/3 tbsp soy sauce
30 ml/2 tbsp dry sherry or vermouth
15 ml/1 tbsp sesame oil
sesame seeds, to sprinkle

Soy Vegetables – stir-fry the leeks, carrots, courgettes and baby corn in the oil for about 2 minutes then add the mushrooms and cook for a further minute. Mix together the soy sauce, sherry and sesame oil and pour over the vegetables. Heat until bubbling then scatter over the sesame seeds.

CHEESY CREAMED CORN FILLING
1 × 425 g/15 oz can creamed corn
115 g/4 oz cheese, grated
5 ml/1 tsp dried mixed herbs

Cheesy creamed corn – heat the corn, add the cheese and mixed herbs.

Peanut Butter Fingers

Children will love these crispy, tasty croquettes. Make up a batch and freeze some ready for whenever there are young tummies to fill!

MAKES 12
1 kg/2 lb potatoes
1 large onion, chopped
2 large peppers, red or green, chopped
3 carrots, coarsely grated
45 ml/3 tbsp sunflower oil
2 courgettes, coarsely grated
115 g/4 oz mushrooms, chopped
15 ml/1 tbsp dried mixed herbs
115 g/4 oz mature Cheddar cheese, grated
75 g/3 oz/½ cup crunchy peanut butter
salt and ground black pepper
2 eggs, beaten
about 50 g/2 oz/½ cup dried breadcrumbs
45 ml/3 tbsp dried Parmesan cheese
oil, for deep frying

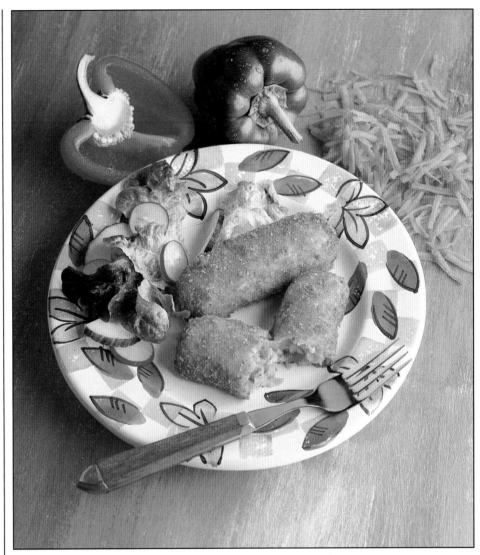

1 Boil the potatoes until tender, then drain well and mash. Set aside.

2 Fry the onion, peppers and carrots gently in the oil for about 5 minutes then add the courgettes and mushrooms. Cook for 5 minutes more.

3 Mix the potato with the dried mixed herbs, grated cheese and peanut butter. Season, allow to cool for 30 minutes, then stir in one of the eggs.

4 Spread out on a large plate, cool and chill, then divide into 12 portions and shape. Dip your hands in cold water if the mixture sticks.

5 Put the second egg in a bowl and dip the potato fingers into it first, then into the crumbs and Parmesan cheese until coated evenly. Return to the fridge to set.

6 Heat oil in a deep fat frier to 190°C/375°F then fry the fingers in batches for about 3 minutes until golden. Drain well on kitchen paper towel. Serve hot.

COOK'S TIP

To reheat, thaw for about 1 hour, then grill or oven bake at 190°C/375°F/Gas 5 for 15 minutes.

Pasta Salade Tiède

Boil a pan of pasta shapes and toss with vinaigrette dressing and some freshly prepared salad vegetables and you have the basis for a delicious warm salad.

SERVES 2
115 g/4 oz pasta shapes, e.g. shells
45 ml/3 tbsp vinaigrette dressing
3 sun-dried tomatoes in oil, snipped
2 spring onions, sliced
25 g/1 oz/2 or 3 sprigs watercress or rocket, chopped
¼ cucumber, halved, seeded and sliced
salt and ground black pepper
about 40 g/1½ oz Pecorino cheese, coarsely grated

1 Boil the pasta according to the instructions on the packet. Drain and toss in the dressing.

2 Mix in the tomatoes, onions, cress or rocket and cucumber. Season to taste.

3 Divide between two plates and sprinkle over the cheese. Eat at room temperature, if possible.

Penne with 'Can Can' Sauce

The quality of canned pulses and tomatoes is so good that it is possible to transform them into a very fresh tasting pasta sauce in minutes. Again, choose whatever pasta you like.

SERVES 3–4
225 g/8 oz penne pasta
1 onion, sliced
1 red pepper, seeded and sliced
30 ml/2 tbsp olive oil
1 × 400 g/14 oz can chopped tomatoes
1 × 425 g/15 oz can chick peas
30 ml/2 tbsp dry vermouth (optional)
5 ml/1 tsp dried oregano
1 large bay leaf
30 ml/2 tbsp capers
salt and ground black pepper

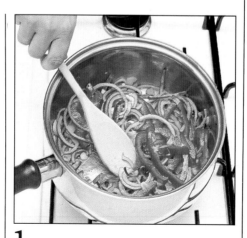

1 Boil the pasta as instructed on the package, then drain. In a saucepan, gently fry the onion and pepper in the oil for about 5 minutes, stirring occasionally, until softened.

2 Add the tomatoes, chick peas with their liquor, vermouth (if liked), herbs and capers.

3 Season and bring to a boil then simmer for about 10 minutes. Remove the bay leaf and mix in the pasta, reheat and serve hot.

Tofu and Crunchy Vegetables

High protein, wonder food tofu is nicest if marinated lightly before cooking. If you use the smoked tofu, it's even tastier. For successful stir-frying, make sure all your ingredients are prepared first.

SERVES 4

2 × 225 g/8 oz cartons smoked tofu, cubed
45 ml/3 tbsp soy sauce
30 ml/2 tbsp dry sherry or vermouth
15 ml/1 tbsp sesame oil
45 ml/3 tbsp groundnut or sunflower oil
2 leeks, thinly sliced
2 carrots, cut in sticks
1 large courgette, thinly sliced
115 g/4 oz baby sweetcorn, halved
115 g/4 oz button or shiitake mushrooms, sliced
15 ml/1 tbsp sesame seeds
1 packet of egg noodles, cooked

1 Marinate the tofu in the soy sauce, sherry or vermouth and sesame oil for at least half an hour. Drain and reserve the marinade.

2 Heat the groundnut or sunflower oil in a wok and stir-fry the tofu cubes until browned all over. Remove and reserve.

3 Stir-fry the leeks, carrots, courgette and baby corn, stirring and tossing for about 2 minutes. Add the mushrooms and cook for a further minute.

4 Return the tofu to the wok and pour in the marinade. Heat until bubbling, then scatter over the sesame seeds.

5 Serve as soon as possible with the hot cooked noodles, dressed in a little sesame oil, if liked.

VARIATION

Tofu is also excellent marinated and skewered, then lightly grilled. Push the tofu off the skewers into pockets of pitta bread. Fill with lemon-dressed salad and serve with a final trickle of tahini cream.

Egg Foo Yung

A great way of turning a bowl of leftover cooked rice into a meal for four, this Oriental dish is tasty and full of texture. Use bought beansprouts or grow your own – it's easy and fun.

SERVES 4

salt and ground black pepper
3 eggs, beaten
good pinch five spice powder (optional)
45 ml/3 tbsp groundnut or sunflower oil
4 spring onions, sliced
1 garlic clove, crushed
1 small green pepper, seeded and
  chopped
115 g/4 oz fresh bean sprouts
225 g/8 oz/3 cups cooked white rice
45 ml/3 tbsp light soy sauce
15 ml/1 tbsp sesame oil

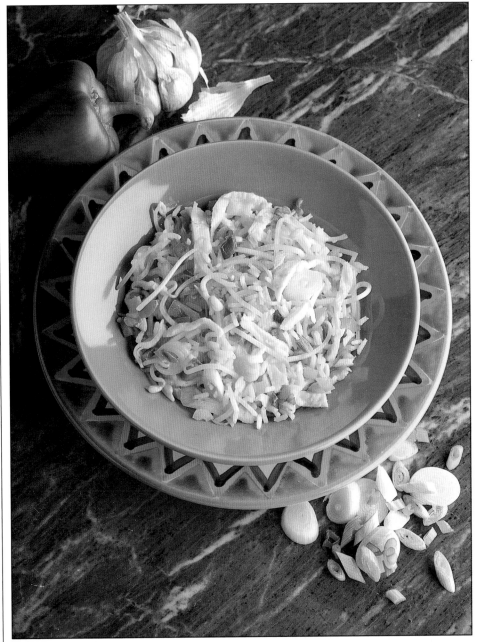

1 Season the eggs and beat in the five spice powder, if using.

2 In a wok or large frying pan, heat one tablespoon of the oil and when quite hot, pour in the egg.

3 Cook rather like an omelette, pulling the mixture away from the sides and allowing the rest to slip underneath.

4 Cook the egg until firm then tip out. Chop the 'omelette' into small strips.

5 Heat the remaining oil and stir-fry the onion, garlic, pepper and bean sprouts for about 2 minutes, stirring and tossing continuously.

6 Mix in the rice and heat thoroughly, stirring well. Add the soy sauce and sesame oil then return the egg and mix in well. Serve immediately, piping hot.

Eggs Benedict with Quick Hollandaise

Traditional Hollandaise sauce is tricky to make without it curdling. To make it quickly, yet still achieve a thick and creamy sauce, use a blender or food processor. Hollandaise sauce is simply delicious served over poached eggs on hot toasted muffins.

SERVES 4
2 egg yolks
5 ml/1 tsp dry mustard
good pinch each salt and ground black
    pepper
15 ml/1 tbsp wine vinegar or lemon juice
175 g/6 oz/¾ cup butter
4 muffins, split
butter or low fat spread
4 large eggs
30 ml/2 tbsp capers
a little fresh parsley, chopped, to garnish

1 Blend the egg yolks with the mustard and seasoning in a blender or food processor for a few seconds until well mixed. Mix in the vinegar or lemon juice.

2 Heat the butter until it is on the point of bubbling then, with the machine still running, slowly pour the butter onto the egg yolks.

3 The mixture should emulsify instantly and become thick and creamy. Switch off the blender and set the sauce aside.

4 Toast the split muffins. Cut four of the halves in two and lightly butter. Place the four uncut halves on warmed plates and leave unbuttered.

5 Poach the eggs either in gently simmering water or in an egg poacher. Drain well and slip carefully onto the muffin halves.

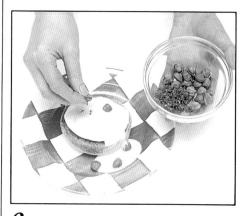

6 Spoon the sauce over the muffins and then sprinkle with capers and parsley. Serve immediately with the buttered muffin quarters.

VARIATION

This classic American brunch dish is said to have originated in New York, and is ideal to serve on a special occasion such as a birthday treat or New Year's day.

Instead of the toasted muffin, you could make more of a main meal by serving the dish on a bed of lightly steamed or blanched spinach mixed with quick fried sliced mushrooms and onions. The quick Hollandaise sauce is of course ideal as an all-purpose serving sauce for vegetables, baked potatoes, cauliflower and broccoli.

Light Ratatouille

This lightly cooked medley of fresh vegetables is cooked with simple poached eggs and served topped with crisply fried breadcrumbs.

SERVES 4
45 ml/3 tbsp olive oil
50 g/2 oz/1 cup fresh white breadcrumbs
1 yellow or red pepper, seeded and thinly sliced
2 garlic cloves, crushed
2 leeks, thinly sliced
2 courgettes, thinly sliced
2 tomatoes, skinned and sliced
5 ml/1 tsp dried rosemary, crushed
4 eggs
salt and ground black pepper

1 Heat half the oil in a shallow fireproof dish (or frying pan with a lid) and fry the breadcrumbs until they are golden and crisp. Drain on kitchen paper towel.

2 Add the remaining oil and fry the pepper, garlic and leeks in the same pan for about 10 minutes until softened.

3 Add the courgettes, tomatoes and rosemary and cook for a further 5 minutes. Season well.

4 Using the back of a spoon, make four wells in the vegetable mixture and break an egg into each one. Lightly season the eggs then cover and cook on a gentle heat for about 3 minutes until they are just set.

5 Sprinkle over the crisp breadcrumbs and serve immediately, piping hot.

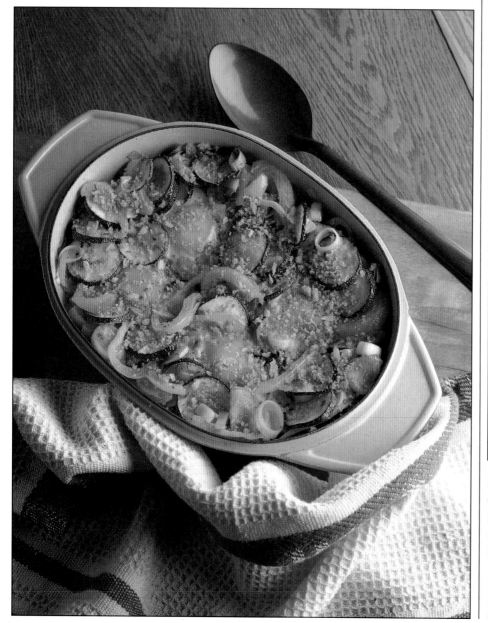

Macaroni Soufflé

This is generally a great favourite with children, and is rather like a light and fluffy macaroni cheese. Make sure you serve a soufflé immediately it is cooked or it will sink dramatically.

SERVES 3–4
75 g/3 oz short cut macaroni
melted butter, to coat
25 g/1 oz/3 tbsp dried breadcrumbs
50 g/2 oz/4 tbsp butter
5 ml/1 tsp ground paprika
40 g/1½ oz/⅓ cup plain flour
300 ml/½ pint/1¼ cups milk
75 g/3 oz Cheddar or Gruyère cheese, grated
50 g/2 oz Parmesan cheese, grated
salt and ground black pepper
3 eggs, separated

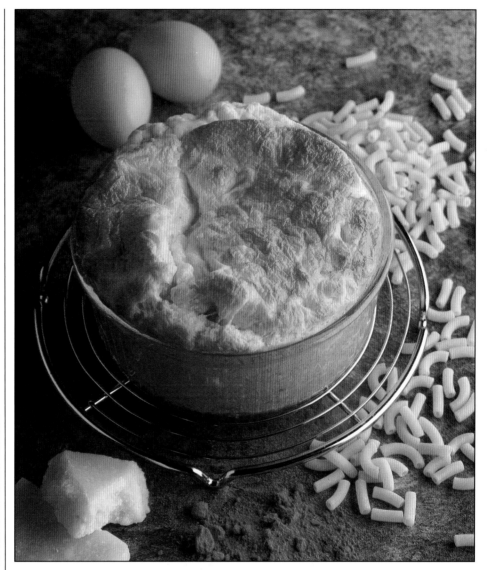

1 Boil the macaroni according to the instructions on the pack. Drain well and then set aside. Preheat the oven to 150°C/300°F/Gas 2.

2 Brush the insides of a 1.2 litre/2 pint soufflé dish with melted butter then coat evenly with the breadcrumbs, shaking out any excess.

3 Put the butter, paprika, flour and milk into a saucepan and bring to the boil slowly, whisking it constantly until it is smooth and thick.

4 Simmer the sauce for a minute, then take off the heat and stir in the cheeses until they melt. Season well and mix with the macaroni.

5 Beat in the egg yolks. Whisk the egg whites until they form soft peaks and spoon a quarter into the sauce mixture, beating it gently to loosen it up.

6 Using a large metal spoon, carefully fold in the rest of the egg whites and transfer to the prepared soufflé dish.

7 Bake in the centre of the oven for about 40–45 minutes until the soufflé has risen and is golden brown. The middle should wobble very slightly and the soufflé should be lightly creamy inside.

Cowboy Hot Pot

A great dish to serve as a children's main meal, which adults will enjoy too – if they are allowed to join the posse. You can use any vegetable mixture you like; although beans are a must for every self-respecting cowboy!

SERVES 4–6
1 onion, sliced
1 red pepper, sliced
1 sweet potato or 2 carrots, chopped
45 ml/3 tbsp sunflower oil
115 g/4 oz green beans, chopped
1 × 400 g/14 oz can baked beans
1 × 200 g/7 oz can sweet corn
15 ml/1 tbsp tomato purée
5 ml/1 tsp barbecue spice seasoning
115 g/4 oz cheese (preferably smoked), cubed
450 g/1 lb potatoes, thinly sliced
25 g/1 oz/2 tbsp butter, melted
salt and ground black pepper

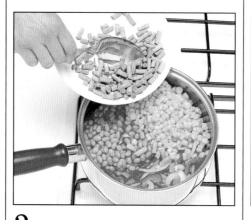

1 Fry the onion, pepper and sweet potato or carrots gently in the oil until softened but not browned.

2 Add the green beans, baked beans, sweetcorn (and liquor), tomato purée and barbecue spice seasoning. Bring to a boil then simmer for 5 minutes.

3 Transfer the vegetables to a shallow ovenproof dish and then scatter with the cubed cheese.

4 Cover the vegetable and cheese mixture with the sliced potato, brush with butter, season and bake at 190°C/375°F/Gas 5 for 30–40 minutes until golden brown on top and the potato is cooked.

Stir-fry Rice and Vegetables 🍃

If you have some left-over cooked rice and a few vegetables lurking at the bottom of the refrigerator, then you've got the basis for this quick and tasty meal.

SERVES 4
½ cucumber
2 spring onions, sliced
1 garlic clove, crushed
2 carrots, thinly sliced
1 small red or yellow pepper, seeded and sliced
45 ml/3 tbsp sunflower or groundnut oil
¼ small green cabbage, shredded
225 g/8 oz/4 cups cooked long grain rice
30 ml/2 tbsp light soy sauce
15 ml/1 tbsp sesame oil
salt and ground black pepper
fresh parsley or coriander, chopped (optional)
115 g/4 oz unsalted cashew nuts, almonds or peanuts

1 Halve the cucumber lengthways and scoop out the seeds with a teaspoon. Slice the flesh diagonally. Set aside.

2 In a wok or large frying pan, stir-fry the onions, garlic, carrots and pepper in the oil for about 3 minutes until they are just soft.

3 Add the cabbage and cucumber and fry for another minute or two until the leaves begin to just wilt. Mix in the rice, soy sauce, sesame oil and seasoning. Reheat the mixture thoroughly, stirring and tossing all the time.

4 Add the herbs, if using, and nuts. Check the seasoning and serve piping hot.

Pepper and Potato Tortilla

A great favourite with my family, tortilla is rather like a thick omelette or pastry-less quiche. Traditionally a Spanish dish, it is best eaten cold in chunky wedges. Tortilla makes ideal picnicking food. Use a hard Spanish cheese, like Mahon, or a goats' cheese, if you can, although mature Cheddar makes a good substitute.

SERVES 4
2 medium size potatoes
45 ml/3 tbsp olive oil
1 large onion, thinly sliced
2 garlic cloves, crushed
2 peppers, one green and one red, thinly
  sliced
6 eggs, beaten
115 g/4 oz mature cheese, grated
salt and ground black pepper

1 Do not peel the potatoes, but wash them thoroughly. Par-boil them as they are for about 10 minutes, then drain and slice them thickly. Switch on the grill so that it has time to warm up while you prepare the tortilla.

2 In a large non-stick or well seasoned frying pan, heat the oil and fry the onion, garlic and peppers on a moderate heat for 5 minutes until softened.

3 Add the potatoes and continue frying, stirring occasionally until the potatoes are completely cooked and the vegetables are soft. Add a little extra oil if the pan seems rather dry.

4 Pour in half the eggs, then sprinkle over half the cheese then the rest of the egg, seasoning as you go. Finish with a layer of cheese.

5 Continue to cook on a low heat, without stirring, half covering the pan with a lid to help set the eggs.

6 When the mixture is firm, flash the pan under the hot grill to just lightly seal the top. Leave the tortilla in the pan to cool. This helps it firm up further and makes it easier to turn out.

VARIATION

You can add any sliced and lightly cooked vegetable, such as mushrooms, courgettes or broccoli, to this tortilla dish instead of peppers. Cooked pasta or brown rice are both excellent alternatives too.

Cauliflower and Egg Cheese

No need to make a traditional bechamel sauce for this country classic. A quick all-in-one sauce can be made in minutes while a small pack of soup croûtons gives the dish a delicious crunchy topping.

SERVES 4

1 medium size cauliflower, broken in
   florets
1 medium onion, sliced
2 eggs, hard boiled, peeled and chopped
40 g/1½ oz/3 tbsp wholemeal flour
5 ml/1 tsp mild curry powder
25 g/1 oz/2 tbsp sunflower margarine or
   low fat spread
450 ml/¾ pint/2 cups milk
2.5 ml/½ tsp dried thyme
salt and ground black pepper
115 g/4 oz mature cheese, grated
small packet of soup croûtons

1 Boil the cauliflower and onion in enough salted water to cover until they are just tender. Be careful not to overcook them. Drain well.

2 Arrange the cauliflower and onion in a shallow ovenproof dish and scatter over the chopped egg.

3 Put the flour, curry powder, fat and milk in a saucepan all together. Bring slowly to the boil, stirring well until thickened and smooth. Stir in the thyme and seasoning and allow the sauce to simmer for a minute or two. Remove the pan from the heat and stir in about three quarters of the cheese.

4 Pour the sauce over the cauliflower, scatter over the croûtons and sprinkle with the remaining cheese. Brown under a hot grill until golden and serve. Delicious with thick crusty bread.

Quick Basmati and Nut Pilaff

Light and fragrant basmati rice from the foothills of the Himalayas cooks perfectly using this simple pilaff method. Use whatever nuts are your favourite – even unsalted peanuts are good, although almonds, cashews or pistachios are more exotic.

SERVES 4–6
225 g/8 oz/1¼ cups basmati rice
1 onion, chopped
1 garlic clove, crushed
1 large carrot, coarsely grated
15–30 ml/1–2 tbsp sunflower oil
5 ml/1 tsp cumin seeds
10 ml/2 tsp ground coriander
10 ml/2 tsp black mustard seeds (optional)
4 cardamom pods
450 ml/¾ pint/2 cups stock or water
1 bay leaf
salt and ground black pepper
75 g/3 oz/½ cup unsalted nuts
fresh chopped parsley or coriander,
   to garnish

RINSING BASMATI

For light, fluffy grains basmati rice is best rinsed before cooking to remove any surface starch. The traditional method is to put the rice into a large bowl of cold water. Swill the grains around with your hands then tip out the cloudy water. (The rice will quickly sink to the bottom.) Repeat this action about five times. Ideally, leave the rice to soak for 30 minutes in the last rinsing water. This ensures a lighter, fluffier grain.

1 Wash the rice either by the traditional Indian method (see note) or in a sieve under a running tap. If there is time, soak the rice for 30 minutes, then drain well in a sieve.

2 In a large shallow pan, gently fry the onion, garlic and carrot in the oil for a few minutes.

3 Stir in the rice and spices and cook for a further minute or two so that the grains are coated in oil.

4 Pour in the stock or water, add the bay leaf and season well. Bring to a boil, cover and simmer very gently for about 10 minutes.

5 Remove from the heat without lifting the lid – this helps the rice to firm up and cook further. Leave for about 5 minutes.

6 If the rice is cooked, there will be small steam holes in the centre. Discard the bay leaf and cardamom pods.

7 Stir in the nuts and check the seasoning. Scatter the mixture with the chopped parsley or coriander. This whole dish can be made ahead and reheated.

Quorn with Ginger, Chilli and Leeks 🌿

Quorn is a newly-developed, versatile mycoprotein food which easily absorbs different flavours and retains a good firm texture. This makes it ideal for stir-frying. It is available in most supermarkets.

SERVES 4

225 g/8 oz Quorn cubes
45 ml/3 tbsp soy sauce
30 ml/2 tbsp dry sherry or vermouth
10 ml/2 tsp clear honey
150 ml/¼ pint/⅔ cup stock
10 ml/2 tsp cornflour
45 ml/3 tbsp sunflower or groundnut oil
3 leeks, thinly sliced
1 red chilli, seeded and sliced
2.5 cm/1 in piece fresh root ginger, peeled and shredded
salt and ground black pepper

1 Toss the Quorn in the soy sauce and sherry or vermouth until well coated and leave to marinate for about 30 minutes.

2 Strain the Quorn from the marinade and reserve the juices in a jug. Mix the marinade with the honey, stock and cornflour to make a paste.

3 Heat the oil in a wok or large frying pan and when hot, stir-fry the Quorn until it is crisp on the outside. Remove the Quorn and set aside.

4 Reheat the oil and stir-fry the leeks, chilli and ginger for about 2 minutes until they are just soft. Season lightly.

5 Return the Quorn to the pan, together with the marinade, and stir well until the liquid is thick and glossy. Serve hot with rice or egg noodles.

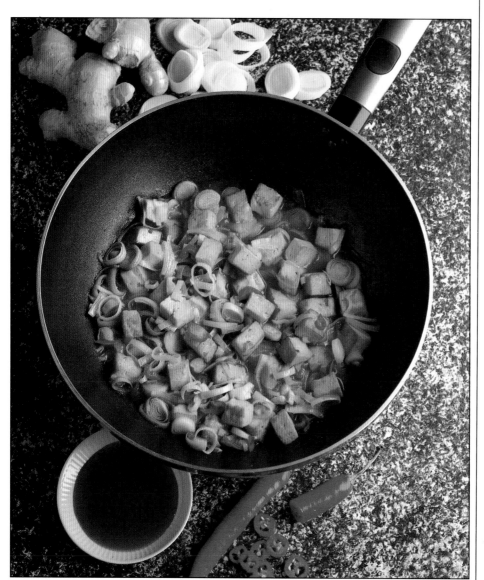

Chinese Potatoes with Chilli Beans 🥬

East meets West. An American style dish with a Chinese flavour – the sauce is particularly tasty. Try it as a quick supper dish when you fancy a meal with a little zing!

SERVES 4

4 medium potatoes, cut in thick chunks
3 spring onions, sliced
1 large fresh chilli, seeded and sliced
30 ml/2 tbsp sunflower or groundnut oil
2 garlic cloves, crushed
1 × 400 g/14 oz can red kidney beans, drained
30 ml/2 tbsp soy sauce
15 ml/1 tbsp sesame oil

TO SERVE

salt and ground black pepper
15 ml/1 tbsp sesame seeds
fresh coriander or parsley, chopped, to garnish

1 Boil the potatoes until they are just tender. Take care not to overcook them. Drain and reserve.

2 In a large frying pan or wok, stir-fry the onions and chilli in the oil for about 1 minute then add the garlic and fry for a few seconds longer.

3 Add the potatoes, stirring well, then the beans and finally the soy sauce and sesame oil.

4 Season to taste and cook the vegetables until they are well heated through. Sprinkle with the sesame seeds and the coriander or parsley.

Tabbouleh 🍃

Almost the ultimate quick grain salad that simply needs soaking, draining and mixing. Bulgur is par-boiled wheat. Make this a day ahead, if possible, so that the flavours have time to develop.

SERVES 4
115 g/4 oz/¾ cup bulgur wheat
90 ml/6 tbsp fresh lemon juice
75 ml/5 tbsp extra virgin olive oil
90 ml/6 tbsp fresh parsley, chopped
60 ml/4 tbsp fresh mint, chopped
3 spring onions, finely chopped
4 firm tomatoes, skinned and chopped
salt and ground black pepper

1 Cover the bulgur with cold water and soak for 20 minutes, then drain well and squeeze out even more water from it with your hands.

2 Put the bulgur into another bowl and add all the other ingredients, stirring and seasoning well.

3 Cover and chill for a few hours, overnight, if possible.

Crudités with Houmous 🍃

Always a great family favourite, homemade houmous is speedily made with the help of a blender. The tahini paste is the secret of houmous and it is readily available in delicatessens or larger supermarkets.

SERVES 2–3
1 × 425 g/15 oz can chick peas, drained
30 ml/2 tbsp tahini paste
30 ml/2 tbsp fresh lemon juice
1 garlic clove, crushed
salt and ground black pepper
olive oil and paprika pepper, to garnish
TO SERVE
Selection of salad vegetables, e.g. cucumber, chicory, baby carrots, pepper strips, radishes
Bite size chunks of bread, e.g. pitta, walnut, naan, bruscheta, or grissini sticks

1 Put the chick peas, tahini paste, lemon juice, garlic and plenty of seasoning into a food processor or blender and mix to a smooth paste.

2 Spoon the houmous into a bowl and swirl the top with the back of a spoon. Trickle over a little olive oil and sprinkle with paprika.

3 Prepare a selection of fresh salad vegetables and chunks of your favourite fresh bread or grissini sticks into finger size pieces.

4 Set out in a colourful jumble on a large plate with the bowl of houmous in the centre. Then dip and eat!

Pitta Pizzas

Pitta breads make very good bases for quick thin and crispy pizzas, and they are easy to eat with your hands too. The perfect speedy snack.

SERVES 4

BASIC PIZZAS
4 pitta breads, ideally wholemeal
small jar of pasta sauce
225 g/8 oz Mozzarella cheese, sliced or grated
dried oregano or thyme, to sprinkle
salt and ground black pepper

EXTRA TOPPINGS – CHOOSE FROM
1 small red onion, thinly sliced and lightly fried
mushrooms, sliced and fried
1 × 200 g/7 oz can sweetcorn, drained
jalapeno chillis, sliced
black or green olives, stoned and sliced
capers, drained

1 Prepare two or three toppings of your choice for the pizzas.

2 Preheat the grill and lightly toast the pitta breads on each side.

3 Spread pasta sauce on each pitta, right to the edge. This prevents the edges of the pitta from burning.

4 Arrange cheese slices or grated cheese on top of each pitta and sprinkle with herbs and seasoning.

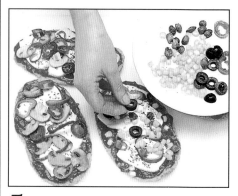

5 Add the toppings of your choice and then grill the pizzas for about 5–8 minutes until they are golden brown and bubbling. Serve immediately.

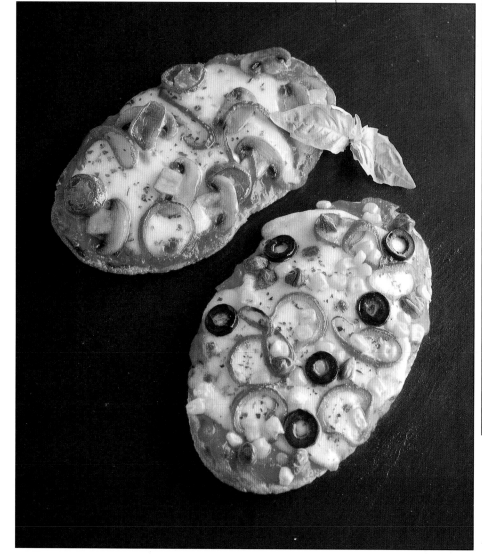

Tagliatelle with Spinach and Soy Garlic Cheese

It's wonderful to mix ingredients from different cuisines and produce a delicious dish as a result. Italian pasta and spinach combine with Chinese soy and French garlic cream cheese to create this wonderful rich and mouth-watering dish.

SERVES 4

225 g/8 oz tagliatelle, preferably mixed colours
225 g/8 oz fresh leaf spinach
30 ml/2 tbsp light soy sauce
75 g/3 oz garlic and herb cheese
45 ml/3 tbsp milk
salt and ground black pepper

1 Boil the tagliatelle according to the instructions on the pack and drain. Return the pasta to the pan.

2 Meanwhile blanch the spinach in a tiny amount of water until just wilted, then drain very well, squeezing dry with the back of a wooden spoon. Chop roughly with kitchen scissors.

3 Return the spinach to its pan and stir in the soy sauce, garlic and herb cheese and milk. Bring slowly to a boil, stirring until smooth. Season to taste.

4 When the sauce is ready, pour it over the pasta. Toss the pasta and sauce together well and serve hot.

Spaghetti with Feta

We think of pasta as being essentially Italian but, in fact, the Greeks have a great appetite for it too and it complements beautifully the tangy, full-flavoured feta cheese.

SERVES 2–3
115 g/4 oz spaghetti
1 garlic clove
30 ml/2 tbsp extra virgin olive oil
8 cherry tomatoes, halved
a little freshly grated nutmeg
salt and ground black pepper
75 g/3 oz feta cheese, crumbled
15 ml/1 tbsp chopped fresh basil
a few black olives (optional), to serve

1 Boil the spaghetti in plenty of lightly salted water according to the instructions on the pack, then drain.

2 In the same pan gently heat the garlic clove in the oil for a minute or two then add the cherry tomatoes.

3 Increase the heat to fry the tomatoes lightly for a minute, then remove the garlic and discard.

4 Toss in the spaghetti, season with the nutmeg and seasoning to taste then stir in the crumbled feta and basil.

5 Check the seasoning, remembering that feta can be quite salty, and serve hot topped with olives if liked.

Potatoes with Blue Cheese and Walnuts

We are so used to eating potatoes as a side dish, we forget they can be a good main meal too. This dish is so versatile it can be served as either. Use Stilton, Danish blue, Blue Brie or any other blue veined cheese.

SERVES 4
450 g/1 lb small new potatoes
small head of celery, sliced
small red onion, sliced
115 g/4 oz blue cheese, mashed
150 ml/¼ pint/⅔ cup single cream
salt and ground black pepper
100 g/3½ oz/½ cup walnut pieces
30 ml/2 tbsp fresh parsley, chopped

1 Cover the potatoes with water and boil for about 15 minutes, adding the sliced celery and onion to the pan for the last 5 minutes or so.

2 Drain the vegetables and put them into a shallow serving dish.

3 In a small saucepan melt the cheese in the cream, slowly, stirring occasionally. Do not allow the mixture to boil but heat it until it scalds.

4 Season the sauce to taste. Pour it over the vegetables and scatter over the walnuts and parsley. Serve hot.

Aduki Bean Burgers

Although not quick to make, these burgers are a delicious alternative to shop-bought ones; so it is worth making up several batches for the freezer. Make sure you use an ordinary long-grain brown rice and not a quick-cook variety.

MAKES 12
200 g/7 oz/1 cup brown rice
1 onion, chopped
2 garlic cloves, crushed
30 ml/2 tbsp sunflower oil
50 g/2 oz/4 tbsp butter
1 small green pepper, seeded and
  chopped
1 carrot, coarsely grated
1 × 400 g/14 oz can aduki beans, drained
  (or 125 g/4 oz dried weight, soaked
  and cooked)
1 egg, beaten
125 g/4 oz mature cheese, grated
5 ml/1 tsp dried thyme
50 g/2 oz/½ cup roasted hazelnuts or
  toasted flaked almonds
salt and ground black pepper
wholemeal flour or cornmeal, for coating
oil, for deep frying

1 Cook the rice according to the instructions on the pack, allowing it to slightly overcook so that it is softer. Strain the rice and transfer it to a large bowl.

2 Fry the onion and garlic in the oil and butter together with the green pepper and carrot for about 10 minutes until the vegetables are softened.

3 Mix this vegetable mixture into the rice, together with the aduki beans, egg, cheese, thyme, nuts or almonds and plenty of seasoning. Chill until quite firm.

4 Shape into 12 patties, using wet hands if the mixture sticks. Coat the patties in flour or cornmeal and set aside.

5 Heat 1 cm/½ in oil in a large, shallow frying pan and fry the burgers in batches until browned on each side, about five minutes in total. Remove and drain on kitchen paper. Eat some burgers freshly cooked, and freeze the rest for later. Serve in buns with salad and relish.

COOK'S TIP

To freeze the burgers, cool them after cooking, then open freeze them before wrapping and bagging. Use within six weeks. Cook from frozen by baking in a pre-heated moderately hot oven for 20–25 minutes.

Courgette Quiche

If possible, use a hard goats' cheese for this flan as its flavour complements the courgettes nicely. Bake the pastry base blind for a crisp crust.

SERVES 6
PASTRY
115 g/4 oz/scant 1 cup wholemeal flour
115 g/4 oz/1 cup plain flour
115 g/4 oz/½ cup sunflower margarine
FILLING
1 red onion, thinly sliced
30 ml/2 tbsp olive oil
2 large courgettes, sliced
175 g/6 oz cheese, grated
30 ml/2 tbsp fresh basil, chopped
3 eggs, beaten
300 ml/½ pint/1¼ cups milk
salt and ground black pepper

1 Preheat the oven to 200°C/400°F/ Gas 6. Mix the flours together and rub in the margarine until it resembles crumbs then mix to a firm dough with cold water.

2 Roll out the pastry and use it to line a 23–25 cm/9–10 in flan tin, ideally at least 2.5 cm/1 in deep. Prick the base, chill for 30 minutes then fill with paper or foil and baking beans.

3 Bake the pastry case blind on a baking sheet for 20 minutes uncovering it for the last 5 minutes so that it can crisp up.

4 Meanwhile, sweat the onion in the oil for 5 minutes, until it is soft. Add the courgettes and fry for another 5 minutes.

5 Spoon the onion and courgettes into the pastry case. Scatter over most of the cheese and all of the basil.

6 Beat together the eggs, milk and seasoning and pour over the filling. Top with the remaining cheese.

7 Turn the oven down to 180°C/350°F/ Gas 4 and return the flan for about 40 minutes until risen and just firm to the touch in the centre. Allow to cool slightly before serving.

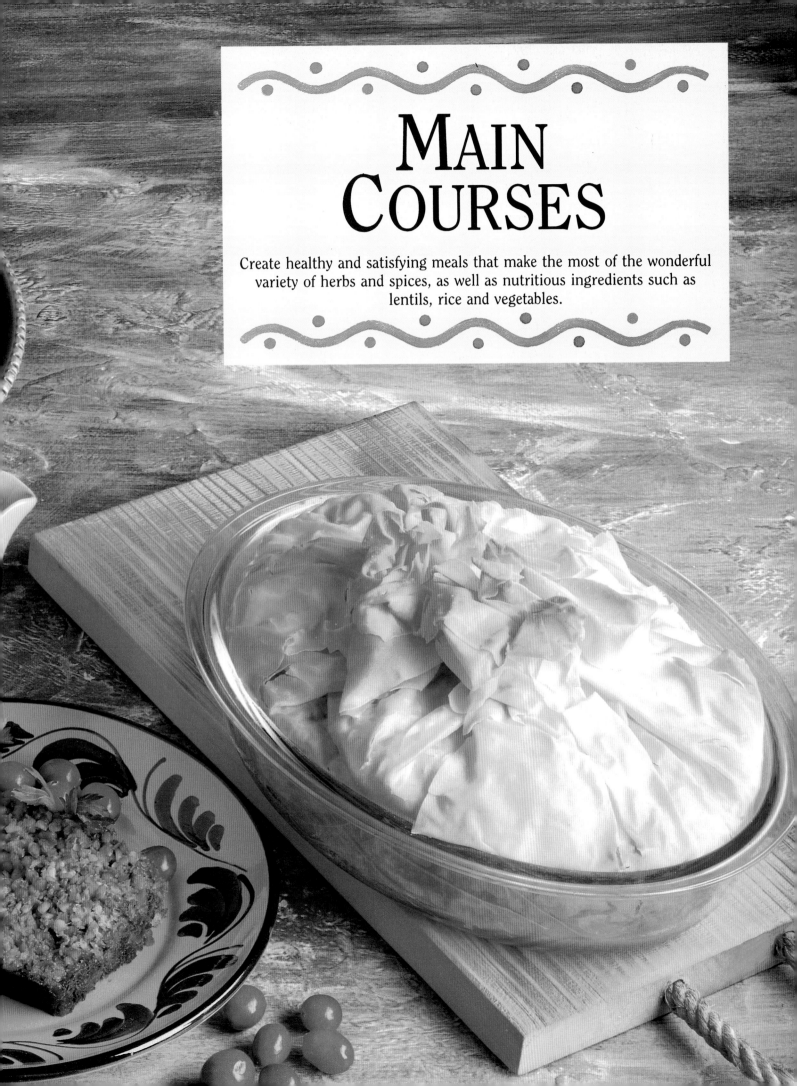

MAIN COURSES

Create healthy and satisfying meals that make the most of the wonderful variety of herbs and spices, as well as nutritious ingredients such as lentils, rice and vegetables.

Arabian Spinach

Stir-fry spinach with onions and spices, then mix in a can of chick peas and you have a delicious family main course meal in next to no time.

SERVES 4
1 onion, sliced
30 ml/2 tbsp olive or sunflower oil
2 garlic cloves, crushed
400 g/14 oz spinach, washed and shredded
5 ml/1 tsp cumin seeds
1 × 425 g/15 oz can chick peas, drained
knob of butter
salt and ground black pepper

1 In a large frying pan or wok, fry the onion in the oil for about 5 minutes until softened. Add the garlic and cumin seeds, then fry for another minute.

2 Add the spinach, in stages, stirring it until the leaves begin to wilt. Fresh spinach condenses down dramatically on cooking and it *will* all fit into the pan.

3 Stir in the chick peas, butter and seasoning. Reheat until just bubbling, then serve hot. Drain off any pan juices, if you like, but this dish is rather nice served slightly saucy.

Vegetable Medley with Lentil Bolognese 🌿

Instead of a white or cheese sauce, it makes a nice change to top a selection of lightly steamed vegetables with a healthy and delicious lentil sauce.

SERVES 6
1 small cauliflower, in florets
225 g/8 oz broccoli florets
2 leeks, thickly sliced
225 g/8 oz Brussels sprouts, halved if large
Lentil Bolognese Sauce

1 Make up the sauce and keep warm.

2 Place all the vegetables in a steamer over a pan of boiling water and cook for 8–10 minutes until just tender.

3 Drain and place in a shallow serving dish. Spoon the sauce on top, stirring slightly to mix. Serve hot.

Falafels

Made with ground chick peas, herbs and spices, falafels are a Middle Eastern street food normally served tucked into warm pitta breads with scoopfuls of salad. They are absolutely delicious served with tahini cream or dollops of natural yogurt.

MAKES 8
1 × 425 g/15 oz can chick peas, drained
1 garlic clove, crushed
30 ml/2 tbsp fresh parsley, chopped
30 ml/2 tbsp fresh coriander, chopped
15 ml/1 tbsp fresh mint, chopped
5 ml/1 tsp cumin seeds
30 ml/2 tbsp fresh breadcrumbs
5 ml/1 tsp salt
ground black pepper
oil, for deep frying

1 Grind the chick peas in a food processor until they are just smooth, then mix them with all the other ingredients until you have a thick, creamy paste. Add pepper to taste.

2 Using wet hands, shape the chick pea mixture into 8 rounds and chill for 30 minutes so that they become firm.

3 Meanwhile, heat about 5 mm/¼ in of oil in a shallow frying pan and fry the falafels a few at a time. Cook each one for about 8 minutes, turning the falafels carefully just once.

4 Drain the falafels on kitchen paper towel and fry the rest in batches, reheating the oil in between. Serve tucked inside warm pitta breads with sliced salad, tomatoes and tahini cream or yogurt.

> **COOK'S TIP**
>
> Falafels can be made in batches and frozen. Allow them to cool, spread out on wire cooling racks and open freeze until solid. Tip into a freezer-proof plastic container. To reheat, bake in a moderate oven for 10–15 minutes.

Caribbean Rice and Peas

A great family favourite in West Indian culture, this dish is not only very tasty, but nutritionally well balanced too. Serve with the gravy sauce and slices of fried aubergine.

SERVES 4
225 g/8 oz/1¼ cups easy-cook long grain
  rice
115 g/4 oz/¾ cup dried gunga peas or red
  kidney beans, soaked and cooked but
  still firm
750 ml/1¼ pints/3⅔ cups water
50 g/2 oz creamed coconut, chopped
5 ml/1 tsp dried thyme or 15 ml/1 tbsp
  fresh thyme leaves
1 small onion stuck with 6 whole cloves
salt and ground black pepper

1 Put the rice and peas or kidney beans into a large saucepan with the water, coconut, thyme, onion and seasoning.

2 Bring to the boil, stirring until the coconut melts then cover and simmer gently for 20 minutes.

3 Remove the lid and allow to cook uncovered for 5 minutes to reduce down any excess liquid. Remove from the heat and stir occasionally to separate the grains. The rice should be quite dry.

Greek Stuffed Vegetables

Vegetables such as peppers make wonderful containers for savoury fillings. Instead of sticking to one type of vegetable, follow the Greeks' example and serve an interesting selection. Thick, creamy Greek yogurt is the ideal accompaniment.

SERVES 3–6
1 medium aubergine
1 large green pepper
2 large tomatoes
1 large onion, chopped
2 garlic cloves, crushed
45 ml/3 tbsp olive oil
200 g/7 oz/1 cup brown rice
600 ml/1 pint/2½ cups stock
75 g/3 oz/¾ cup pine nuts
50 g/2 oz/⅓ cup currants
salt and ground black pepper
45 ml/3 tbsp fresh dill, chopped
45 ml/3 tbsp fresh parsley, chopped
15 ml/1 tbsp fresh mint, chopped
extra olive oil, to sprinkle
natural Greek yogurt, to serve
fresh sprigs of dill

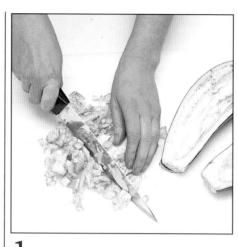

1 Halve the aubergine, scoop out the flesh with a sharp knife and chop finely. Salt the insides and leave to drain upside down for 20 minutes while you prepare the other ingredients.

2 Halve the pepper, seed and core. Cut the tops from the tomatoes, scoop out the insides and chop roughly along with the tomato tops.

3 Fry the onion, garlic and chopped aubergine in the oil for 10 minutes, then stir in the rice and cook for 2 minutes.

4 Add the tomato flesh, stock, pine nuts, currants and seasoning. Bring to the boil, cover and simmer for 15 minutes then stir in the fresh herbs.

5 Blanch the aubergine and green pepper halves in boiling water for about 3 minutes, then drain them upside down.

6 Spoon the rice filling into all six vegetable 'containers' and place on a lightly greased ovenproof shallow dish.

7 Heat the oven to 190°C/375°F/Gas 5, drizzle over some olive oil and bake the vegetables for 25–30 minutes. Serve hot, topped with spoonfuls of natural yogurt and dill sprigs.

Red Onion and Courgette Pizza

It's easy to make a homemade pizza using one of the new fast-action yeasts. You can either add the traditional cheese and tomato topping or try something different, such as the one described here.

SERVES 4
350 g/12 oz/3 cups plain flour
1 sachet fast action/easy blend yeast
10 ml/2 tsp salt
lukewarm water to mix
TOPPING
2 red onions, thinly sliced
60 ml/4 tbsp olive oil
2 courgettes, thinly sliced
salt and ground black pepper
fresh nutmeg, grated
about 115 g/4 oz semi-soft goats' cheese
6 sun-dried tomatoes in oil, snipped
dried oregano
extra olive oil, to sprinkle

1 Preheat the oven to 200°C/400°F/ Gas 6. Mix the flour, yeast and salt together, then mix to a firm dough with warm water. How much depends on the flour, but start with 150 ml/¼ pint.

2 Knead the dough for about 5 minutes until it is smooth and elastic then roll it out to a large circle and place on a lightly greased baking sheet.

3 Set the base aside somewhere warm to rise slightly while you make the topping.

4 Gently fry the onions in half the oil for 5 minutes then add the courgettes and fry for a further 2 minutes. Season and add nutmeg to taste.

5 Spread the pizza base with fried vegetable mixture and dot with the cheese, tomatoes and oregano. Sprinkle over the rest of the olive oil and bake for 12–15 minutes until golden and crisp.

Sprouting Beans and Pak Choi 🌿

Supermarkets are fast becoming cosmopolitan and many stock ethnic fresh vegetables.

SERVES 4
45 ml/3 tbsp groundnut oil
3 spring onions, sliced
2 garlic cloves, cut in slivers
2.5 cm/1 in cube fresh root ginger, cut in slivers
1 carrot, cut in thin sticks
150 g/5 oz sprouting beans (e.g. lentils, mung beans, chick peas)
1 × 200 g/7 oz pak choi cabbage, shredded
50 g/2 oz/½ cup unsalted cashew nuts or halved almonds
SAUCE
45 ml/3 tbsp light soy sauce
30 ml/2 tbsp dry sherry
15 ml/1 tbsp sesame oil
150 ml/¼ pint/⅔ cup cold water
5 ml/1 tsp cornflour
5 ml/1 tsp clear honey
ground black pepper

1 Heat the oil in a large wok and stir-fry the onions, garlic, ginger and carrot for 2 minutes. Add the sprouting beans and fry for another 2 minutes, stirring and tossing them together.

2 Add the pak choi and nuts or almonds and stir-fry until the cabbage leaves are just wilting. Quickly mix all the sauce ingredients together in a jug and pour them into the wok, stirring immediately.

3 The vegetables will be coated in a thin, glossy sauce. Season and serve as soon as possible.

Thai Tofu Curry 🌿

Thai food is a marvellous mixture of Chinese and Indian styles, plus other exotic ingredients.

SERVES 4
2 × 200 g/7 oz packs tofu curd, cubed
30 ml/2 tbsp light soy sauce
30 ml/2 tbsp groundnut oil
PASTE
1 small onion, chopped
2 fresh green chillies, seeded and chopped
2 garlic cloves, chopped
15 ml/1 tbsp grated gresh gallingale or 5 ml/1 tsp grated fresh ginger
2 Thai kaffir leaves or 5 ml/1 tsp lime rind, grated
10 ml/2 tsp coriander berries, crushed
10 ml/2 tsp cumin seeds, crushed
45 ml/3 tbsp fresh coriander, chopped
15 ml/1 tbsp Thai fish sauce (Nam pla) or soy sauce
juice of 1 lime or small lemon
5 ml/1 tsp sugar
25 g/1 oz creamed coconut dissolved in 150 ml/¼ pint/⅔ cup boiling water
GARNISH
thin slices fresh red chilli or red pepper
fresh coriander leaves

1 Toss the tofu cubes in soy sauce and leave to marinate for 15 minutes or so while you prepare the paste.

2 Put all the paste ingredients into a food processor and grind until smooth.

3 To cook, heat the oil in a wok until quite hot. Drain the tofu cubes and stir fry at a high temperature until well browned on all sides and just firm. Drain on kitchen paper towel.

4 Wipe out the wok. Pour in the paste and stir well. Return the tofu to the wok and mix it into the paste, reheating the ingredients as you stir.

5 Serve this dish on a flat platter garnished with red chilli or pepper and chopped coriander. Bowls of Thai fragrant or jasmine rice are the perfect accompaniment to the curry.

Festive Jalousie

An excellent puff pastry pie to serve either on Christmas Day or at anytime during the holiday period. Chinese dried chestnuts make an excellent substitute for fresh ones when soaked and cooked. Or you could drain a can of chestnuts.

SERVES 6
450 g/1 lb puff pastry, thawed if frozen
450 g/1 lb Brussels sprouts, trimmed
about 16 whole chestnuts, peeled if fresh
1 large red pepper, sliced
1 large onion, sliced
45 ml/3 tbsp sunflower oil
1 egg yolk, beaten with 15 ml/1 tbsp
    water
SAUCE
40 g/1½ oz/scant ½ cup plain flour
40 g/1½ oz/3 tbsp butter
300 ml/½ pint/1¼ cups milk
75 g/3 oz Cheddar cheese, grated
30 ml/2 tbsp dry sherry
good pinch dried sage
salt and ground black pepper
45 ml/3 tbsp fresh parsley, chopped

1 Roll out the pastry to make two large rectangles, roughly the size of your dish. The pastry should be about 6 mm/¼ in thick and one rectangle should be slightly larger than the other. Set the pastry aside in the refrigerator.

2 Blanch the Brussels sprouts for 4 minutes in 300 ml/½ pint/1¼ cups boiling water then drain, reserving the water. Refresh the sprouts under cold running water.

3 Cut each chestnut in half. Lightly fry the red pepper and onion in the oil for 5 minutes. Set aside till later.

4 Make up the sauce by beating the flour, butter and milk together over a medium heat. Beat the sauce continuously, bringing it to the boil, stirring until it is thickened and smooth.

5 Stir in the reserved sprout water, and the cheese, sherry, sage and seasoning. Simmer for 3 minutes to reduce and mix in the parsley.

6 Fit the larger piece of pastry into your pie dish and layer the sprouts, chestnuts, peppers and onions on top. Trickle over the sauce, making sure it seeps through to wet the vegetables.

7 Brush the pastry edges with beaten egg yolk and fit the second pastry sheet on top, pressing the edges well to seal them.

8 Crimp, knock up the edges then mark the centre. Glaze well all over with egg yolk. Set aside to rest somewhere cool while you preheat the oven to 200°C/400°F/Gas 6. Bake for 30–40 minutes until golden brown and crisp.

Shepherdess Pie

A no-meat version of the timeless classic, this dish also has no dairy products in it, so it is suitable for vegans. However, you can serve it with confidence to anyone wanting a hearty meal.

SERVES 6—8
1 kg/2 lb potatoes
45 ml/3 tbsp extra virgin olive oil
salt and ground black pepper
1 large onion, chopped
1 green pepper, chopped
2 carrots, coarsely grated
2 garlic cloves
45 ml/3 tbsp sunflower oil or margarine
115 g/4 oz mushrooms, chopped
2 × 400 g/14 oz cans aduki beans, drained
600 ml/1 pint/2½ cups stock
5 ml/1 tsp vegetable yeast extract
2 bay leaves
5 ml/1 tsp dried mixed herbs
dried breadcrumbs or chopped nuts, to sprinkle

1 Boil the potatoes in the skins until tender, then drain, reserving a little of the water to moisten them.

2 Mash well, mixing in the olive oil and seasoning until you have a smooth purée. (Potatoes are easier to peel when boiled in their skins. This also preserves vitamins.)

3 Gently fry the onion, pepper, carrots and garlic in the sunflower oil or margarine for about 5 minutes until they are soft. Preheat the grill.

4 Stir in the mushrooms and beans and cook for a further 2 minutes, then add the stock, yeast extract, bay leaves and mixed herbs. Simmer for 15 minutes.

5 Remove the bay leaves and empty the vegetables into a shallow ovenproof dish. Spoon on the potatoes in dollops and sprinkle over the crumbs or nuts. Grill until golden brown.

Magnificent Marrow

At autumn time, marrows – with their wonderful green and cream stripes – look so attractive and tempting. They make delicious, inexpensive main courses, just right for a satisfying family Sunday lunch.

SERVES 4–6
250 g/8 oz/3 cups pasta shells
1.5–1.75 kg/3–4 lb marrow
1 onion, chopped
1 pepper, seeded and chopped
15 ml/1 tbsp fresh root ginger, grated
2 garlic cloves, crushed
45 ml/3 tbsp sunflower oil
4 large tomatoes, skinned and chopped
salt and ground black pepper
50 g/2 oz/½ cup pine nuts
15 ml/1 tbsp fresh basil, chopped
cheese, grated, to serve (optional)

1 Preheat the oven to 190°C/375°F/ Gas 5. Boil the pasta according to the instructions on the pack, slightly overcooking it so it is just a little soft. Drain and reserve.

2 Cut the marrow in half lengthways and scoop out the seeds. These can be discarded. Use a small sharp knife and tablespoon to scoop out the marrow flesh. Chop the flesh roughly.

3 Gently fry the onion, pepper, ginger and garlic in the oil for 5 minutes then add the marrow flesh, tomatoes and seasoning. Cover and cook for 10–12 minutes until the vegetables are soft.

4 Add to the pan the pasta, pine nuts and basil, stir well and set aside.

5 Meanwhile, place the marrow halves in a roasting pan, season lightly and pour a little water around the marrow, taking care it does not spill inside. Cover with foil and bake for 15 minutes.

6 Remove the foil, discard the water and fill the shells with the vegetable mixture. Recover with foil and return to the oven for a further 20–25 minutes.

7 If you wish, serve this dish topped with grated cheese. The marrow can either be served cut into sections or scooped out of the 'shell'.

Greek Spinach Pies

These little horns of filo pastry are stuffed with a simple spinach and feta cheese filling to make a quick and easy main course.

SERVES 8
225 g/8 oz fresh leaf spinach
2 spring onions, chopped
175 g/6 oz feta cheese, crumbled
1 egg, beaten
15 ml/1 tbsp fresh dill, chopped
ground black pepper
4 large sheets or 8 small sheets of filo pastry
olive oil, for brushing

COOK'S TIP

The pies can be prepared ahead and chilled for a day or two, before baking and serving warm. Alternatively, open freeze on a wire rack, then wrap well in foil or cling film and freeze for up to one month. Uncover and thaw well before baking as the recipe above.

1 Preheat the oven to 190°C/375°F/ Gas 5. Blanch the spinach in the tiniest amount of water until just wilted, then drain very well, pressing it through a sieve with the back of a wooden spoon.

2 Chop the spinach finely and mix with the onions, feta, egg, dill and ground black pepper.

3 Lay out a sheet of filo pastry and brush with olive oil. If large, cut the pieces in two and sandwich them together. If small, fit another sheet on top and brush with olive oil.

4 Spread a quarter of the filling on one edge of the filo at the bottom, then roll it up firmly, but not too tightly. Shape into a crescent and place on a baking sheet.

5 Brush the pastry well with oil and bake for about 20–25 minutes in the preheated oven until golden and crisp. Cool slightly then remove to a wire rack to cool further.

Chunky Vegetable Paella

This Spanish rice dish has become a firm family favourite the world over. There are very many versions: here is one with aubergine and chick peas.

SERVES 6
good pinch saffron strands
1 aubergine, cut in thick chunks
salt
90 ml/6 tbsp olive oil
1 large onion, sliced
3 garlic cloves, crushed
1 yellow pepper, sliced
1 red pepper, sliced
10 ml/2 tsp paprika
225 g/8 oz/1¼ cups risotto rice
600 ml/1 pint/2½ cups stock
450 g/1 lb fresh tomatoes, skinned and chopped
ground black pepper
115 g/4 oz sliced mushrooms
115 g/4 oz cut green beans
1 × 400 g/14 oz can chick peas

1 Steep the saffron in 45 ml/3 tbsp hot water. Sprinkle the aubergine with salt, leave to drain in a colander for 30 minutes, then rinse and dry.

2 In a large paella or frying pan, heat the oil and fry the onion, garlic, peppers and aubergine for about 5 minutes, stirring occasionally. Sprinkle in the paprika and stir again.

3 Mix in the rice, then pour in the stock, tomatoes, saffron and seasoning. Bring to a boil then simmer for 15 minutes, uncovered, shaking the pan frequently and stirring occasionally.

4 Stir in the mushrooms, green beans and chick peas (with the liquor). Continue cooking for a further 10 minutes, then serve hot from the pan.

Green Lentil Kulbyaka

This traditional Russian dish, usually made with fish and dough, can be adapted to make a light, crisp vegetarian centrepiece using filo pastry and green lentils.

SERVES 6

175 g/6 oz/1 cup green lentils, soaked for 30 minutes
2 bay leaves
2 onions, sliced
1.2 litres/2 pints/5 cups stock
175 g/6 oz/¾ cup butter, melted
225 g/8 oz/1¼ cups long grain rice, ideally basmati
salt and ground black pepper
60 ml/4 tbsp fresh parsley, chopped
30 ml/2 tbsp fresh dill, chopped
1 egg, beaten
225 g/8 oz mushrooms, sliced
about 8 sheets filo pastry
3 eggs, hard-boiled and sliced

---

1 Drain the lentils then simmer with the bay leaves, one onion and half the stock for 25 minutes until cooked and thick. Season well, cool and set aside.

VARIATION

You could use a vegetarian puff pastry. In this case, use two blocks of pastry, placing one on top of the other and rolling to a large rectangle. Alternatively, you could make two separate kulbyakas. Divide the filling between the pastry and seal the edges well, glazing the tops with beaten egg.

2 Gently fry the remaining onion in another saucepan with 30 ml/2 tbsp of the butter for 5 minutes. Stir in the rice then the rest of the stock.

3 Season, bring to the boil, then cover and cook gently for 12 minutes for basmati, 15 minutes for long grain. Leave to stand, uncovered for 5 minutes then stir in the fresh herbs. Cool, then beat in the raw egg.

4 Fry the mushrooms in 45 ml/3 tbsp of the butter for 5 minutes until they are just soft. Cool and set aside.

5 Brush the inside of a large, shallow ovenproof dish with more butter. Lay the sheets of filo in it, covering the base and making sure most of the pastry overhangs the sides. Brush well with butter in between and overlapping the pastry as required. Ensure there is a lot of pastry to fold over the mounded filling.

6 Into the pastry lining, layer rice, lentils and mushrooms, repeating the layers at least once and tucking the sliced egg in between. Season as you layer and form an even mound of filling.

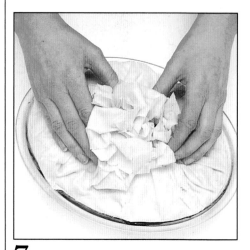

7 Bring up the sheets of pastry over the filling, scrunching the top into attractive folds. Brush all over with the rest of the butter and set aside to chill and firm up.

8 Preheat the oven to 190°C/375°F/ Gas 5. When ready, bake the kulbyaka for about 45 minutes until golden and crisp. Allow to stand for 10 minutes before you cut it and serve.

Turnip and Chick Pea Cobbler

A good mid-week meal with an attractive savoury scone topping. Use a star shape cutter for the topping.

SERVES 4–6
1 onion, sliced
2 carrots, chopped
3 medium size turnips, chopped
1 small sweet potato or swede, chopped
2 celery sticks, sliced thinly
45 ml/3 tbsp sunflower oil
2.5 ml/½ tsp ground coriander
2.5 ml/½ tsp dried mixed herbs
1 × 425 g/15 oz can chopped tomatoes
1 × 400 g/14 oz can chick peas
1 vegetable stock cube
salt and ground black pepper
TOPPING
225 g/8 oz/2 cups self-raising flour
5 ml/1 tsp baking powder
50 g/2 oz/4 tbsp margarine
45 ml/3 tbsp sunflower seeds
30 ml/2 tbsp Parmesan cheese, grated
150 ml/¼ pint/⅔ cup milk

1 Fry all the vegetables in the oil for about 10 minutes until they are soft. Add the coriander, herbs, tomatoes, chick peas with their liquor and stock cube. Season well and simmer for 20 minutes.

2 Pour the vegetables into a shallow casserole dish while you make the topping. Preheat the oven to 190°C/375°F/Gas 5.

3 Mix together the flour and baking powder then rub in the margarine until it resembles fine crumbs. Stir in the seeds and Parmesan cheese. Add the milk and mix to a firm dough.

4 Lightly roll out the topping to a thickness of 1 cm/½ in and stamp out star shapes or rounds, or simply cut it into small squares.

5 Place the shapes on top of the vegetable mixture and brush with a little extra milk. Bake for 12–15 minutes until risen and golden brown. Serve hot with green, leafy vegetables.

Tangy Fricassé

Vegetables in a light tangy sauce and covered with a crispy crumb topping make a simple and easy main course to serve with crusty bread and salad.

SERVES 4
4 courgettes, sliced
115 g/4 oz green beans, sliced
4 large tomatoes, skinned and sliced
1 onion, sliced
50 g/2 oz/4 tbsp butter or sunflower
    margarine
40 g/1½ oz/⅓ cup plain flour
10 ml/2 tsp coarse grain mustard
450 ml/¾ pint/2 cups milk
150 ml/¼ pint/⅔ cup natural yogurt
5 ml/1 tsp dried thyme
115 g/4 oz mature cheese, grated
salt and ground black pepper
60 ml/4 tbsp fresh wholemeal
    breadcrumbs tossed with 15 ml/1 tbsp
    sunflower oil

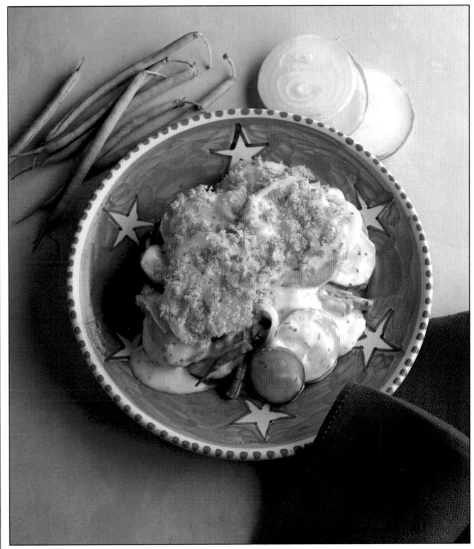

1 Blanch the courgettes and beans in a small amount of boiling water for just 5 minutes then drain and arrange in a shallow ovenproof dish.

2 Arrange all but three slices of tomato on top. Put the onion into a saucepan with the butter or margarine and fry gently for 5 minutes.

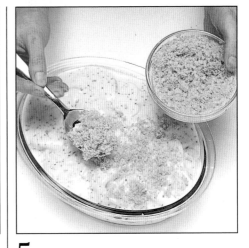

3 Stir in the flour and mustard, cook for a minute then add the milk gradually until the sauce has thickened. Simmer for a further 2 minutes.

4 Remove the pan from the heat, add the yogurt, thyme and cheese, stirring until melted. Season to taste. Reheat gently if you wish, but do not allow the sauce to boil or it will curdle.

5 Pour the sauce over the vegetables and scatter the breadcrumbs on top. Brown under a preheated grill until golden and crisp, taking care not to let them burn. Garnish with the reserved tomato slices if desired.

Chilli con Queso

Known as a 'bowl of red', this classic Mexican dish is just as tasty when made with all-red beans. For an extra good flavour, use small cubes of smoked cheese, and serve with rice. Epazote is a traditional Mexican herb found in specialist stores.

SERVES 4
225 g/8 oz/2 cups red kidney beans, soaked and drained
45 ml/3 tbsp sunflower oil
1 onion, chopped
1 red pepper, chopped
2 garlic cloves, crushed
1 fresh red chilli, chopped (optional)
15 ml/1 tbsp chilli powder (mild or hot)
5 ml/1 tsp ground cumin
1 litre/1¾ pints/4 cups stock or water
5 ml/1 tsp crushed dried epazote leaves (optional)
ground black pepper
salt
15 g/½ oz granulated sugar
115 g/4 oz cheese, cubed, to serve

1 Rinse the beans. In a large saucepan heat the oil and gently fry the onion, pepper, garlic and fresh chilli for about 5 minutes.

2 Stir in the spices and cook for another minute, then add the beans, stock or water, epazote (if using) and a grinding of pepper. Don't add salt at this stage.

3 Boil for 10 minutes, cover and turn down to a gentle simmer. Cook for about 50 minutes checking the water level and adding extra if necessary.

4 When the beans are tender, season them well with salt. Remove about a quarter of the mixture and mash to a pulp or pass through a food processor.

5 Return the purée to the pan and stir well. Add sugar and serve hot with the cheese sprinkled on top. Great with plain boiled long grain rice.

Big Barley Bowl

Barley seems to have slipped from fashion in recent years – a pity as it is a delicious grain with a marvellous nutty texture. Serve this with crisp cheesy croûtes.

SERVES 6
1 red onion, sliced
½ fennel bulb, sliced
2 carrots, cut in sticks
1 parsnip, sliced
45 ml/3 tbsp sunflower oil
115 g/4 oz/1 cup pearl barley
1 litre/1¼ pints/4 cups stock
5 ml/1 tsp dried thyme
fresh parsley, chopped, to garnish
salt and ground black pepper
115 g/4 oz/⅔ cup green beans, sliced
1 × 425 g/15 oz can pinto beans, drained
CROÛTES
1 medium sized baguette, sliced
olive oil, for brushing
1 garlic clove, cut in half
60 ml/4 tbsp grated Parmesan cheese

1 In a large, heatproof casserole, sauté the onion, fennel, carrots and parsnip gently in the oil for 10 minutes.

2 Stir in the barley and stock. Bring to a boil, add the herbs and seasoning, then cover and simmer gently for 40 minutes.

3 Stir in the green beans and pinto beans and continue cooking – covered – for a further 20 minutes.

4 Meanwhile, preheat the oven to 190°C/375°F/Gas 5. Brush the baguette slices with olive oil and place them on a baking sheet.

5 Bake for about 15 minutes until light golden and crisp. Remove from the oven and quickly rub each croûte with the garlic halves. Sprinkle over the cheese and return to the oven to melt.

6 Ladle the barley into warm bowls and serve sprinkled with parsley, accompanied by the cheesy croûtes. This dish is nicest eaten with a spoon.

Vegetables Julienne with a Red Pepper Coulis

Just the right course for those watching their weight. Choose a selection of as many vegetables as you feel you can eat. Cut them into equal size finger lengths and steam them over aromatic, bubbling water.

SERVES 2

A selection of vegetables. Choose from:
  carrots, turnips, asparagus, parsnips,
  courgettes, green beans, broccoli,
  salsify, cauliflower, mangetouts

RED PEPPER COULIS

1 small onion, chopped
1 garlic clove, crushed
15 ml/1 tbsp sunflower oil
15 ml/1 tbsp water
3 red peppers, roasted, skinned and
  chopped
120 ml/8 tbsp fromage frais
squeeze of fresh lemon juice
salt and ground black pepper
sprigs of fresh thyme
2 bay leaves
fresh green herbs, to garnish

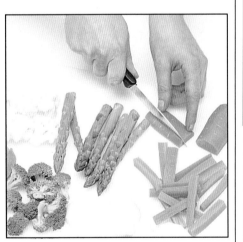

1 Prepare the vegetables by cutting them into thin fingers or small, bite size pieces.

2 Make the coulis: lightly sauté the onion and garlic in the oil and water for 3 minutes then add the peppers and cook for a further 2 minutes.

3 Pass the coulis through a food processor, then work in the fromage frais, lemon juice and seasoning.

4 Boil some salted water with the fresh thyme and bay leaves, and fit a steamer over the top.

5 Arrange the prepared vegetables on the steamer, placing the harder root vegetables at the bottom and steaming these for about 3 minutes.

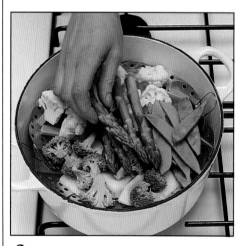

6 Add the other vegetables according to their natural tenderness and cook for a further 2–4 minutes.

7 Serve the vegetables on plates with the sauce to one side. Garnish with fresh green herbs, if you wish.

VARIATION

The red pepper coulis makes a wonderful sauce for many other dishes. Try it spooned over fresh pasta with lightly steamed or fried courgettes, or use it as a pouring sauce for savoury filled crêpes.

Pistachio Pilaff in a Spinach Crown 🍂

Saffron and ginger are traditional rice spices and even more delicious when mixed with fresh pistachio nuts. This is a particularly good, light main course needing just a tomato salad for accompaniment.

SERVES 4
3 onions
60 ml/4 tbsp olive oil
2 garlic cloves, crushed
2.5 cm/1 in cube fresh root ginger, grated
1 fresh green chilli, chopped
2 carrots, coarsely grated
225 g/8 oz/1¼ cups basmati rice, rinsed
1.25 ml/¼ tsp saffron strands, crushed
450 ml/¾ pint/2 cups stock
1 cinnamon stick
5 ml/1 tsp ground coriander
salt and ground black pepper
75 g/3 oz/¼ cup fresh pistachio nuts
450 g/1 lb fresh leaf spinach
5 ml/1 tsp garam masala powder

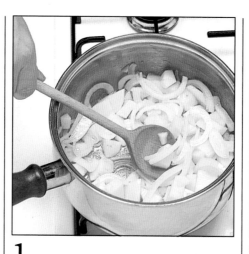

1 Roughly chop two of the onions. Heat half the oil in a large saucepan and fry the onion with half the garlic, the ginger and the chilli for 5 minutes.

2 Mix in the carrots and rice, cook for 1 more minute and then add the saffron, stock, cinnamon and coriander. Season well. Bring to a boil, then cover and simmer gently for 10 minutes, without lifting the lid.

3 Remove from the heat and leave to stand, uncovered, for 5 minutes. Add the pistachio nuts, mixing them in with a fork. Remove the cinnamon stick and keep the rice warm.

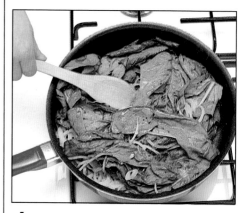

4 Thinly slice the third onion and fry in the remaining oil for about 3 minutes. Stir in the spinach. Cover and cook for another 2 minutes.

5 Add the garam masala powder. Cook until just tender, then drain and roughly chop the spinach.

6 Spoon the spinach round the edge of a round serving dish and pile the pilaff in the centre. Serve hot.

Spinach Bread and Butter Bake

Ideally use Italian ciabatta bread for this, or failing that, a French style baguette. It gives a much lighter bake.

SERVES 4–6
400 g/14 oz fresh leaf spinach
1 ciabatta loaf, thinly sliced
50 g/2 oz/4 tbsp softened butter, olive oil or low fat spread
1 red onion, thinly sliced
115 g/4 oz mushrooms, thinly sliced
30 ml/2 tbsp olive oil
5 ml/1 tsp cumin seeds
salt and ground black pepper
115 g/4 oz Gruyère or Gouda cheese, grated
3 eggs
500 ml/18 fl oz/2¼ cups milk
fresh nutmeg, grated

1 Rinse the spinach well and blanch it in the tiniest amount of water for 2 minutes. Drain well, pressing out any excess water and chop roughly.

2 Spread the bread slices thinly with the butter or low fat spread. Grease a large shallow ovenproof dish and line the base and sides with bread.

3 Fry the onion and mushrooms lightly in the oil for 5 minutes then add the cumin seeds and spinach. Season well.

4 Layer the spinach mixture with the remaining bread and half the cheese. For the top, mix everything together and sprinkle over the remaining cheese.

5 Beat the eggs with the milk, adding seasoning and nutmeg to taste. Pour slowly over the whole dish and set aside for a good hour to allow the custard to be absorbed into the bread.

6 Preheat the oven to 190°C/375°F/Gas 5. Stand the dish in a roasting pan and pour around some boiling water for a bain marie. Bake for 40–45 minutes until risen, golden brown and crispy on top.

Curried Parsnip Pie

Sweet, creamy parsnips are beautifully complemented by the addition of curry spices and cheese. This unusual but delicious combination of flavours makes for a very tasty pie.

SERVES 4
PASTRY
115 g/4 oz/8 tbsp butter or margarine
225 g/8 oz/1 cup plain flour
salt and ground black pepper
5 ml/1 tsp dried thyme or oregano
cold water, to mix
FILLING
8 baby onions, or shallots, peeled
2 large parsnips, thinly sliced
2 carrots, thinly sliced
25 g/1 oz/2 tbsp butter or margarine
30 ml/2 tbsp wholemeal flour
15 ml/1 tbsp mild curry or tikka paste
300 ml/½ pint/1¼ cups milk
115 g/4 oz mature cheese, grated
salt and ground black pepper
45 ml/3 tbsp fresh coriander or parsley, chopped
1 egg yolk, beaten with 10 ml/2 tsp water

1 Make the pastry by rubbing the butter or margarine into the flour until it resembles fine breadcrumbs. Season and stir in the thyme or oregano, then mix to a firm dough with cold water.

2 Blanch the baby onions or shallots with the parsnips and carrots in just enough water to cover, for about 5 minutes. Drain, reserving about 300 ml/ ½ pint/1¼ cups of the liquid.

3 In a clean pan, melt the butter or margarine, and stir in the flour and spice paste to make a roux. Gradually whisk in the reserved stock and milk until smooth. Simmer for a minute or two.

4 Take the pan off the heat, stir in the cheese and seasoning, then mix into the vegetables with the coriander or parsley.

COOK'S TIP

This pie freezes well and makes a good stand-by for a mid-week meal. For best results, make up to the final stage and freeze unbaked. Open freeze until solid, then wrap well in freezer cling film, seal and label. Use within one month.

Cauliflower, broccoli or any other favourite vegetable can be added to the filling to give a variety of flavours and textures.

5 Pour into a pie dish, fix a pie funnel in the centre and allow to cool.

6 Roll out the pastry, large enough to fit the top of the pie dish. Re-roll the trimmings into long strips.

7 Brush the pastry edges with egg yolk wash and fit on the pastry strips. Brush again with egg yolk wash.

8 Using a rolling pin, lift the rolled out pastry over the pie top and fit over the funnel, pressing it down well onto the strips underneath.

9 Cut off the overhanging pastry and crimp the edges. Cut a hole for the funnel, brush all over well with the remaining egg yolk wash and make decorations with the trimmings, glazing them too.

10 Place the pie dish on a baking sheet and chill for 30 minutes while you preheat the oven to 200°C/400°F/Gas 6. Bake the pie for about 25–30 minutes until golden brown and crisp on top.

Vegetables under a Light Creamy Crust

This light main course dish is ideal for a summer supper. The subtle flavours of leeks, courgettes and mushrooms are topped by a tasty crust of fromage frais, cheese and breadcrumbs.

SERVES 4
2 leeks, thinly sliced
3 courgettes, thickly sliced
350 g/12 oz sliced mushrooms, including oyster and shitake mushrooms
2 garlic cloves, crushed
30 ml/2 tbsp olive oil
25 g/1 oz/2 tbsp butter
15 ml/1 tbsp plain flour
300 ml/½ pint/1¼ cups stock
5 ml/1 tsp dried thyme
salt and ground black pepper
30 ml/2 tbsp fromage frais
TOPPING
450 g/1 lb fromage frais
25 g/1 oz/2 tbsp butter, melted
3 eggs, beaten
salt and ground black pepper
fresh nutmeg, grated
freshly grated cheese and dried breadcrumbs, to sprinkle

1 Preheat the oven to 190°C/375°F/Gas 5. In a saucepan, gently fry the leeks, courgettes, mushrooms and garlic in the oil and butter for about 7 minutes, stirring occasionally, until the vegetables are just soft.

2 Stir in the flour then gradually mix in the stock. Bring to a boil, stirring until thickened. Add the thyme and seasoning. Take the pan off the heat and stir in the fromage frais. Pour the vegetable mixture into a shallow ovenproof dish.

3 Beat the topping ingredients together, seasoning them well and adding the nutmeg to taste. Spoon on top of the vegetables and sprinkle with cheese and breadcrumbs.

4 Bake for about 30 minutes until a light golden, firm crust forms. Serve hot with pasta or crusty bread.

Potato and Parsnip Amandine

Shells of baked potatoes are filled with a spicy parsnip and crunchy almond mix. They make an unusual alternative to plain jacket potatoes.

SERVES 4
4 large baking potatoes
olive oil, for greasing
225 g/8 oz parsnips, diced
25 g/1 oz/2 tbsp butter
5 ml/1 tsp cumin seeds
5 ml/1 tsp ground coriander
30 ml/2 tbsp single cream or natural yogurt
salt and ground black pepper
115 g/4 oz Gruyère or Cheddar cheese, grated
1 egg, beaten
50 g/2 oz/¼ cup flaked almonds

1 Rub the potatoes all over with oil, score in half, then bake at 200°C/400°F/Gas 6 for about 1 hour until cooked.

2 Meanwhile, boil the parsnips until tender, then drain well, mash and mix with the butter, spices and cream or natural yogurt.

3 When the potatoes are cooked, halve, scoop out and mash the flesh then mix with the parsnip, seasoning well.

4 Stir in the cheese, egg and three quarters of the almonds. Fill the potato shells with the mixture and sprinkle over the remaining almonds.

5 Return to the oven and bake for about 15–20 minutes until golden brown and the filling has set lightly. Serve hot with a side salad.

Autumn Glory

Glorious pumpkin shells summon up the delights of autumn and seem too good simply to throw away. Use one instead as a serving pot. Pumpkin and pasta make marvellous partners, especially as a main course served from the baked shell.

SERVES 4
1 × 2 kg/4 lb pumpkin
1 onion, sliced
2.5 cm/1 in cube fresh root ginger
45 ml/3 tbsp extra virgin olive oil
1 courgette, sliced
115 g/4 oz sliced mushrooms
1 × 400 g/14 oz can chopped tomatoes
75 g/3 oz/1 cup pasta shells
450 ml/¾ pint/2 cups stock
salt and ground black pepper
60 ml/4 tbsp fromage frais
30 ml/2 tbsp fresh basil, chopped

1 Preheat the oven to 180°C/350°F/Gas 4. Cut the top off the pumpkin with a large, sharp knife and scoop out and discard the seeds.

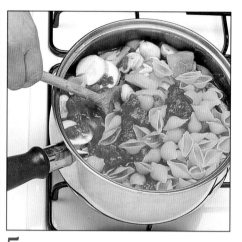

2 Using a small sharp knife and a sturdy tablespoon extract as much of the pumpkin flesh as possible, then chop it into chunks.

3 Bake the pumpkin with its lid on for 45 minutes to one hour until the inside begins to soften.

4 Meanwhile, make the filling. Gently fry the onion, ginger and pumpkin flesh in the olive oil for about 10 minutes, stirring occasionally.

5 Add the courgette and mushrooms and cook for a further 3 minutes, then stir in the tomatoes, pasta shells and stock. Season well, bring to a boil, then cover and simmer gently for 10 minutes.

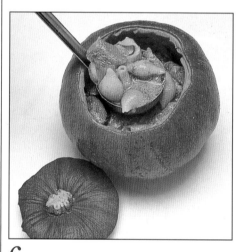

6 Stir the fromage frais and basil into the pasta and spoon the mixture into the pumpkin. (It may not be possible to fit all the filling into the pumpkin shell, so serve the rest separately if this is the case.)

Festive Lentil and Nut Roast

An excellent celebration mould which can be served with all the trimmings, including vegetarian gravy. Garnish it with fresh cranberries and French parsley for a really festive effect.

SERVES 6–8
115 g/4 oz/⅔ cup red lentils
115 g/4 oz/1 cup hazelnuts
115 g/4 oz/1 cup walnuts
1 large carrot
2 celery sticks
1 large onion
115 g/4 oz mushrooms
50 g/2 oz/4 tbsp butter
10 ml/2 tsp mild curry powder
30 ml/2 tbsp tomato ketchup
30 ml/2 tbsp Worcestershire sauce
1 egg, beaten
10 ml/2 tsp salt
60 ml/4 tbsp fresh parsley, chopped
150 ml/¼ pint/⅔ cup water

1 Soak the lentils for 1 hour in cold water then drain well. Grind the nuts in a food processor until quite fine but not too smooth. Set the nuts aside.

2 Chop the carrot, celery, onion and mushrooms into small chunks, then pass them through a food processor or blender until they are quite finely chopped.

3 Fry the vegetables gently in the butter for 5 minutes then stir in the curry powder and cook for a minute. Cool.

4 Meanwhile, mix the soaked lentils with the nuts, vegetables, ketchup, Worcestershire sauce, egg, salt, parsley and water.

5 Grease and line the base and sides of a long 1 kg/2 lb loaf tin with greaseproof paper or a sheet of foil. Press the mixture into the tin. Preheat the oven to 190°C/375°F/Gas 5.

6 Bake for about 1–1¼ hours until just firm, covering the top with a butter paper or piece of foil if it starts to burn.

7 Allow the mixture to stand for about 15 minutes before you turn it out and peel off the paper. It will be fairly soft when cut as it is a moist loaf.

Vegetarian Gravy

Make up a large batch of this and freeze it in small containers ready to reheat and serve. A delicious alternative to the meaty version.

MAKES ABOUT 1 LITRE/1¾ PINTS
1 large red onion, sliced
3 turnips, sliced
3 celery sticks, sliced
115 g/4 oz mushrooms, halved
2 whole garlic cloves
90 ml/6 tbsp sunflower oil
1.5 litres/2½ pints/6 cups vegetable stock
  or water
45 ml/3 tbsp soy sauce
good pinch of granulated sugar
salt and ground black pepper

1 Cook the vegetables and garlic on a moderately high heat with the oil in a large saucepan, stirring occasionally until nicely browned but not singed. This should take about 15–20 minutes.

2 Add the stock or water and soy sauce, bring to the boil then cover and simmer for another 20 minutes.

3 Purée the vegetables, adding a little of the stock, and return them to the pan by rubbing the pulp through a sieve with the back of a ladle or wooden spoon.

4 Taste for seasoning and add the sugar. Freeze at least half of the gravy to use later and reheat the rest to serve with the lentil and nut roast.

Homemade Ravioli

It is a pleasure to make your own fresh pasta and you might be surprised at just how easy it is to fill and shape ravioli. Allow a little extra time than you would for ready-made or dried pasta. A food processor will save you time and effort in making and kneading the dough. A pasta rolling machine helps with the rolling out, but both these jobs can be done by hand if necessary.

SERVES 6
200 g/7 oz/1½ cups strong plain flour
5 ml/½ tsp salt
15 ml/1 tbsp olive oil
2 eggs, beaten
FILLING
1 small red onion, finely chopped
1 small green pepper, finely chopped
1 carrot, coarsely grated
15 ml/1 tbsp olive oil
50 g/2 oz/½ cup walnuts, chopped
115 g/4 oz ricotta cheese
30 ml/2 tbsp fresh Parmesan or Pecorino cheese, grated
15 ml/1 tbsp fresh marjoram or basil, chopped
salt and ground black pepper
extra oil or melted butter, to serve

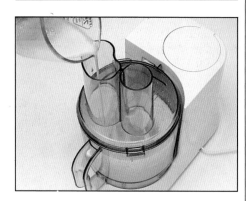

1 Sift the flour and salt into a food processor. With the machine running, trickle in the oil and eggs and blend to a stiff but smooth dough.

2 Allow the machine to run for at least a minute if possible, otherwise remove the dough and knead it by hand for 5 minutes.

3 If you are using a pasta machine, break off small balls of dough and then feed them through the rollers, several times, according to the machine manufacturer's instructions.

4 If rolling the pasta by hand, divide the dough into two and roll out on a lightly floured surface to a thickness of about 6 mm/¼ in.

5 Fold the pasta into three and re-roll. Repeat this up to six times until the dough is smooth and no longer sticky. Roll the pasta slightly more thinly each time.

6 Keep the rolled dough under clean, dry tea towels while you complete the rest and make the filling. You should aim to have an even number of pasta sheets, all the same size if rolling by machine.

7 Fry the onion, pepper and carrot in the oil for 5 minutes, then allow to cool. Mix with the walnuts, cheeses, herbs and seasoning.

8 Lay out a pasta sheet and place small scoops of the filling in neat rows about 5 cm/2 in apart. Brush in between with a little water and then place another pasta sheet on the top.

9 Press down well in between the rows then, using a ravioli or pastry cutter, cut into squares. If the edges pop open occasionally, press them back gently with your fingers.

10 Leave the ravioli to dry in the refrigerator, then boil in plenty of lightly salted water for just 5 minutes.

11 Toss the cooked ravioli in a little oil or melted butter before serving with homemade tomato sauce or extra cheese.

Mushroom Puff Pasties

If possible, use the more full-flavoured chestnut or brown mushrooms for these tasty pasties.

MAKES 8
2 × 225 g/8 oz blocks frozen puff pastry,
   thawed
1 egg, beaten
FILLING
1 onion, chopped
1 carrot, coarsely grated
1 medium potato, coarsely grated
45 ml/3 tbsp sunflower oil
225 g/8 oz sliced mushrooms
30 ml/2 tbsp soy sauce
15 ml/1 tbsp tomato ketchup
15 ml/1 tbsp dry sherry (optional)
good pinch dried thyme
salt and ground black pepper

1 Roll out the pastry blocks until they are 6 mm/¼ in thick and cut each block into four 15 cm/6 in squares. Reserve a little pastry for decoration. Cover the rolled pastry squares and oddments and set aside in a cool place to rest.

2 Make the filling by gently frying the onion, carrot and potato in the oil for 5 minutes, then add the mushrooms, soy sauce, ketchup, sherry (if using), thyme and seasoning.

3 Cook, stirring occasionally, until the mushrooms and vegetables have softened and feel quite tender. Cool.

4 Divide the filling between the eight squares, placing it to one side across the diagonal. Brush the pastry edges with egg then fold over into triangles and press well to seal. From the pastry scraps, cut out little shapes, such as mushrooms, to decorate the pasties.

5 Crimp each pastie edge and top with the cut-out shapes. Set on two baking sheets. Preheat the oven to 200°C/400°F/ Gas 6 and in the meantime allow the pasties to rest somewhere cool.

6 Glaze the pasties with beaten egg, then bake for 15–20 minutes until golden brown and crisp.

Winter Casserole with Herb Dumplings

When the cold weather draws in, gather together a good selection of vegetables and make this comforting casserole with some hearty old-fashioned dumplings.

SERVES 6
2 potatoes
2 carrots
1 small fennel bulb
1 small swede
2 leeks
2 courgettes
50 g/2 oz/4 tbsp butter or margarine
30 ml/2 tbsp plain flour
1 × 425 g/15 oz can butter beans, with liquor
600 ml/1 pint/2½ cups stock
30 ml/2 tbsp tomato purée
1 cinnamon stick
10 ml/2 tsp ground coriander
2.5 ml/½ tsp ground ginger
2 bay leaves
salt and ground black pepper
DUMPLINGS
200 g/7 oz/1½ cups plain flour
115 g/4 oz vegetable suet, shredded, or chilled butter, grated
5 ml/1 tsp dried thyme
5 ml/1 tsp salt
120 ml/4 fl oz/½ cup milk

1 Cut all the vegetables into even, bite size chunks, then fry gently in the butter or margarine for about 10 minutes.

2 Stir in the flour then the liquor from the beans, the stock, tomato purée, spices, bay leaves and seasoning. Bring to the boil, stirring.

3 Cover and simmer for 10 minutes then add the beans and cook for a further 5 minutes.

4 Meanwhile, to make the dumplings, simply mix the flour, suet or butter, thyme and salt to a firm but moist dough with the milk and knead with your hands until it is smooth.

VARIATION

Try chopped walnuts and grated Parmesan or dumplings *fines herbes*. Finely chop ingredients and stir into flour.

5 Divide the dough into 12 pieces, rolling each one into a ball with your fingers. Uncover the simmering stew and then add the dumplings, allowing space between each one for expansion.

6 Replace the lid and cook on a gentle simmer for a further 15 minutes. Do not peek – or you will let out all the steam. Neither should you cook dumplings too fast, or they will break up. Remove the cinnamon stick and bay leaves before you serve this dish, steaming hot.

Lasagne Rolls

Perhaps a more elegant presentation than ordinary lasagne, but just as tasty and popular. You will need to boil 'no-need-to-cook' lasagne as it needs to be soft enough to roll!

SERVES 4
8–10 lasagne sheets
lentil bolognese (see below)
225 g/8 oz fresh leaf spinach
115 g/4 oz mushrooms, sliced
115 g/4 oz Mozzarella cheese, thinly sliced
BECHAMEL SAUCE
40 g/1½ oz/scant ½ cup plain flour
40 g/1½ oz/3 tbsp butter or margarine
600 ml/1 pint/2½ cups milk
bay leaf
salt and ground black pepper
fresh nutmeg, grated
freshly grated Parmesan or Pecorino
   cheese, to serve

Lentil Bolognese

A really useful sauce to serve with pasta, such as lasagne rolls, as a pancake stuffing or even as a protein-packed sauce for vegetables.

SERVES 6
1 onion, chopped
2 garlic cloves, crushed
2 carrots, coarsely grated
2 celery sticks, chopped
45 ml/3 tbsp olive oil
115 g/4 oz/⅔ cup red lentils
1 × 400 g/14 oz can chopped tomatoes
30 ml/2 tbsp tomato purée
450 ml/¾ pint/2 cups stock
15 ml/1 tbsp fresh marjoram, chopped, or
   5 ml/1 tsp dried marjoram
salt and ground black pepper

1 Cook lasagne sheets according to instructions on the pack, or for about 10 minutes. Drain and allow to cool.

2 Cook the spinach in the tiniest amount of water for 2 minutes then add the sliced mushrooms and cook for a further 2 minutes. Drain very well, pressing out all the excess liquor, and chop roughly.

3 Put all the bechamel ingredients into a saucepan and bring slowly to a boil, stirring continuously until the sauce is thick and smooth. Simmer for 2 minutes with the bay leaf then season well and stir in grated nutmeg to taste.

VARIATION

Needless to say, the fillings in this recipe could be any of your own choice. One of my favourites is a lightly stir-fried mixture of colourful vegetables such as peppers, courgettes, aubergines and mushrooms, topped with a cheesy béchamel as above, or with a fresh tomato sauce, which is especially good in summer.

4 Lay out the pasta sheets and spread with the bolognese, spinach and mushrooms and Mozzarella. Roll up each one and place in a large shallow casserole dish with the join face down.

5 Remove and discard the bay leaf and then pour the sauce over the pasta. Sprinkle over the cheese and place under a hot grill to brown.

1 In a large saucepan, gently fry the onion, garlic, carrots and celery in the oil for about 5 minutes, until they are soft.

2 Add the lentils, tomatoes, tomato purée, stock, marjoram and seasoning.

3 Bring the mixture to a boil then partially cover with a lid and simmer for 20 minutes until thick and soft. Use the bolognese as required.

Artichoke and Leek Crêpes

Fill thin pancakes with a mouth-watering soufflé mixture of Jerusalem artichokes and leek to serve for a special main course.

SERVES 4
115 g/4 oz/1 cup plain flour
pinch of salt
1 egg
300 ml/½ pint/1¼ cups milk
oil, for brushing
SOUFFLÉ FILLING
450 g/1 lb Jerusalem artichokes, peeled and diced
1 large leek, sliced thinly
50 g/2 oz/4 tbsp butter
30 ml/2 tbsp self-raising flour
30 ml/2 tbsp single cream
75 g/3 oz mature Cheddar cheese, grated
30 ml/2 tbsp fresh parsley, chopped
fresh nutmeg, grated
2 eggs, separated
salt and ground black pepper

1 Make the crêpe batter by blending the flour, salt, egg and milk to a smooth batter in a food processor or blender.

2 Using a crêpe or omelette pan with a diameter of about 20 cm/8 in, make a batch of thin pancakes. You will need about 30 ml/2 tbsp of batter for each one.

3 Stack the pancakes under a clean tea towel as you make them. Reserve eight for this dish and freeze the rest.

4 Cook the artichokes and leek with the butter in a covered saucepan on a gentle heat for about 12 minutes until very soft. Mash with the back of a wooden spoon. Season well.

5 Stir the flour into the vegetables and cook for 1 minute. Take the pan off the heat and beat in the cream, cheese, parsley and nutmeg to taste. Cool, then add the egg yolks.

6 Whisk the egg whites until they form soft peaks and carefully fold them into the leek/artichoke mixture.

7 Lightly grease a small ovenproof dish and preheat the oven to 190°C/375°F/Gas 5. Fold each pancake in four, hold the top open and spoon the mixture into the centre.

8 Arrange the crêpes in the prepared dish with the filling uppermost if possible. Bake for about 15 minutes until risen and golden. Eat immediately!

COOK'S TIP

Make sure the pan is at a good steady heat and is well oiled before you pour in the batter. It should sizzle as it hits the pan. Swirl the batter round to coat the pan, and then cook quickly.

Broccoli Risotto Torte

Like a Spanish omelette, this is a savoury cake served in wedges. It is good cold or hot, and needs only a salad as an accompaniment.

SERVES 6

225 g/8 oz broccoli, cut into very small florets
1 onion, chopped
2 garlic cloves, crushed
1 large yellow pepper, sliced
30 ml/2 tbsp olive oil
50 g/2 oz/4 tbsp butter
225 g/8 oz/1¼ cups risotto rice
120 ml/4 fl oz/½ cup dry white wine
1 litre/1¾ pints/4½ cups stock
salt and ground black pepper
115 g/4 oz Pecorino or Parmesan cheese, coarsely grated
4 eggs, separated
oil, for greasing
sliced tomato and chopped parsley, to garnish

1 Blanch the broccoli for 3 minutes then drain and reserve.

2 In a large saucepan, gently fry the onion, garlic and pepper in the oil and butter for 5 minutes until they are soft.

3 Stir in the rice, cook for a minute then pour in the wine. Cook, stirring the mixture until the liquid is absorbed.

4 Pour in the stock, season well, bring to the boil then lower to a simmer. Cook for 20 minutes, stirring occasionally.

5 Meanwhile, grease a 25 cm/10 in round deep cake tin and line the base with a disc of greaseproof paper. Preheat the oven to 180°C/350°F/Gas 4.

6 Stir the cheese into the rice, allow the mixture to cool for 5 minutes, then beat in the egg yolks.

7 Whisk the egg whites until they form soft peaks and carefully fold into the rice. Turn into the prepared tin and bake for about 1 hour until risen, golden brown and slightly wobbly in the centre.

8 Allow the torte to cool in the tin, then chill if serving cold. Run a knife round the edge of the tin and shake out onto a serving plate. If liked, garnish with sliced tomato and chopped parsley.

Leek and Chèvre Lasagne

An unusual and lighter than average lasagne using a soft French goats' cheese. The pasta sheets are not so chewy if boiled briefly first. If you do choose no-cook lasagne, then make more sauce to soak into the pasta.

SERVES 6
6–8 lasagne pasta sheets
salt
1 large aubergine
3 leeks, thinly sliced
30 ml/2 tbsp olive oil
2 red peppers, roasted
200 g/7 oz chèvre, broken into pieces
50 g/2 oz Pecorino or Parmesan cheese, freshly grated
SAUCE
60 g/2½ oz/½ cup plain flour
60 g/2½ oz/5 tbsp butter
900 ml/1½ pints/3¾ cups milk
2.5 ml/½ tsp ground bay leaves
fresh nutmeg, grated
ground black pepper

1 Blanch the pasta sheets in plenty of boiling water for just 2 minutes. Drain and place on a clean tea towel.

2 Lightly salt the aubergine and lay in a colander to drain for 30 minutes, then rinse and pat dry with kitchen paper.

3 Lightly fry the leeks in the oil for about 5 minutes until softened. Peel the roasted peppers and cut into strips.

4 Make the sauce: put the flour, butter and milk into a saucepan and bring to the boil, stirring constantly until it has thickened. Add the ground bay leaves, nutmeg and seasoning. Simmer for a further 2 minutes.

5 In a greased shallow casserole, layer the leeks, pasta, aubergine, chèvre and Pecorino or Parmesan. Trickle the sauce over the layers, ensuring that plenty goes in between.

6 Finish with a layer of sauce and grated cheese. Bake in the oven at 190°C/375°F/Gas 5 for 30 minutes or until browned on top. Serve immediately.

Glamorgan Sausages

An old Welsh recipe which tastes particularly good served with creamy mashed potatoes and lightly cooked green cabbage.

SERVES 4

115 g/4 oz/2 cups fresh wholemeal breadcrumbs
150 g/6 oz mature Cheddar or Caerphilly cheese, grated
30 ml/2 tbsp leek or spring onion, finely chopped
30 ml/2 tbsp fresh parsley, chopped
15 ml/1 tbsp fresh marjoram, chopped
15 ml/1 tbsp coarse grain mustard
2 eggs, 1 separated
ground black pepper
50 g/2 oz/½ cup dried breadcrumbs
oil, for deep fat frying

1 Mix the fresh breadcrumbs with the cheese, leek or onion, parsley, marjoram, mustard, whole egg, one egg yolk and ground black pepper to taste. The mixture may appear dry at first but knead it lightly with your fingers and it will come together. Make 8 small sausage shapes.

2 Whisk the egg white until lightly frothy and put the dried breadcrumbs into a bowl. Dip the sausages first into egg white, and then coat them evenly in breadcrumbs, shaking off any excess.

3 Heat a deep fat frying pan a third full of oil and carefully fry four sausages at a time for 2 minutes each. Drain on kitchen paper towel and reheat the oil to repeat.

4 Keep the sausages warm in the oven, uncovered. Alternatively, open freeze, bag and seal, then to reheat, thaw for 1 hour and cook in a moderately hot oven for 10–15 minutes.

Brazilian Stuffed Peppers

Colourful and full of flavour, these stuffed peppers are easy to make in advance. They can be reheated quickly in a microwave oven and browned under a grill.

SERVES 4

4 peppers, halved and seeded
1 aubergine, cut in chunks
1 onion, sliced
1 garlic clove, crushed
30 ml/2 tbsp olive oil
1 × 400 g/14 oz can chopped tomatoes
5 ml/1 tsp ground coriander
salt and ground black pepper
15 ml/1 tbsp fresh basil, chopped
115 g/4 oz goats' cheese, coarsely grated
30 ml/2 tbsp dried breadcrumbs

1 Blanch the pepper halves in boiling water for 3 minutes, then drain well.

2 Sprinkle the aubergine chunks with salt, place in a colander and leave to drain for 20 minutes. Rinse and pat dry.

3 Fry the onion and garlic in the oil for 5 minutes until they are soft, then add the aubergine and cook for a further 5 minutes, stirring occasionally.

VARIATION

There are all sorts of delicious stuffings for peppers. Rice or pasta make a good base, mixed with some lightly fried onion, garlic and spices. Mixed nuts, finely chopped, can be added and a beaten egg or grated cheese helps to bind it all together. Vegans can leave out the last two ingredients.

4 Pour in the tomatoes, coriander and seasoning. Bring to the boil, then simmer for 10 minutes until the mixture is thick. Cool slightly, stir in the basil and half of the cheese.

5 Spoon into the pepper halves and place on a shallow heatproof serving dish. Sprinkle with cheese and breadcrumbs, then brown lightly under the grill. Serve with rice and salad.

Mushroom Gougère

A savoury choux pastry ring makes a marvellous main course dish that can be made ahead then baked when required. Why not try it for a dinner party? It looks so very special.

SERVES 4
115 g/4 oz/½ cup strong plain flour
2.5 ml/½ tsp salt
75 g/3 oz/6 tbsp butter
200 ml/7 fl oz/¾ cup cold water
3 eggs, beaten
75 g/3 oz/¾ cup diced Gruyère or mature Gouda cheese
FILLING
1 small onion, sliced
1 carrot, coarsely grated
225 g/8 oz button mushrooms, sliced
40 g/1½ oz/3 tbsp butter or margarine
5 ml/1 tsp tikka or mild curry paste
25 g/1 oz/2 tbsp plain flour
300 ml/½ pint/1¼ cups milk
30 ml/2 tbsp fresh parsley, chopped
salt and ground black pepper
30 ml/2 tbsp flaked almonds

1 Preheat the oven to 200°C/400°F/Gas 6. Grease a shallow ovenproof dish about 23 cm/9 in long.

2 To make the choux pastry, first sift the flour and salt onto a sheet of greaseproof paper.

3 In a large saucepan, heat the butter and water until the butter just melts. Do not let the water boil. Fold the paper and shoot the flour into the pan all at once.

4 With a wooden spoon, beat the mixture rapidly until the lumps become smooth and the mixture comes away from the sides of the pan. Cool for 10 minutes.

5 Beat the eggs gradually into the mixture until you have a soft, but still quite stiff, dropping consistency. You may not need all the egg.

6 Stir in the cheese, then spoon the mixture round the sides of the greased ovenproof dish.

7 To make the filling, sauté the onion, carrot and mushrooms in the butter or margarine for 5 minutes. Stir in the curry paste then the flour.

8 Gradually stir in the milk and heat until thickened. Mix in the parsley, season well, then pour into the centre of the choux pastry.

9 Bake for 35–40 minutes until risen and golden brown, sprinkling on the almonds for the last 5 minutes or so. Serve at once.

COOK'S TIP

Choux pastry is remarkably easy to make, as no rolling out is required. The secret of success is to let the flour and butter mixture cool before beating in the eggs, to prevent them from setting.

Couscous-stuffed Cabbage

A whole stuffed cabbage makes a wonderful main dish, especially for a Sunday lunch. It can be made ahead and steamed when required. Cut into wedges and serve accompanied by a fresh tomato or cheese sauce or even a vegetarian gravy.

SERVES 4
1 medium size cabbage
115 g/4 oz/1 cup couscous grains
1 onion, chopped
1 small red pepper, chopped
2 garlic cloves, crushed
30 ml/2 tbsp olive oil
5 ml/1 tsp ground coriander
2.5 ml/½ tsp ground cumin
good pinch ground cinnamon
115 g/4 oz/½ cup green lentils, soaked
600 ml/1 pint/2½ cups stock
30 ml/2 tbsp tomato purée
salt and ground black pepper
30 ml/2 tbsp fresh parsley, chopped
30 ml/2 tbsp pine nuts or flaked almonds
75 g/3 oz mature Cheddar cheese, grated
1 egg, beaten

1 Cut the top quarter off the cabbage and remove any loose outer leaves. Using a small sharp knife, cut out as much of the middle as you can. Reserve a few larger leaves for later.

2 Blanch the cabbage in a pan of boiling water for 5 minutes, then drain it well, upside down.

> **VARIATION**
>
> You could substitute healthy brown rice for the couscous.

3 Steam the couscous according to the instructions on the pack, ensuring they are light and fluffy.

4 Lightly fry the onion, pepper and garlic in the oil for 5 minutes until soft then stir in the spices and cook for a further 2 minutes.

5 Add the lentils and pour in the stock and tomato purée. Bring to the boil, season and simmer for 25 minutes until the lentils are cooked.

6 Mix in the couscous, parsley, nuts or almonds, cheese and egg. Check the seasoning again. Open up the cabbage and spoon in the stuffing.

7 Blanch the leftover outer cabbage leaves and place these over the top of the stuffing, then wrap the whole thing in a sheet of buttered foil.

8 Place in a steamer over simmering water and cook for about 45 minutes. Remove from the foil and serve cut into wedges.

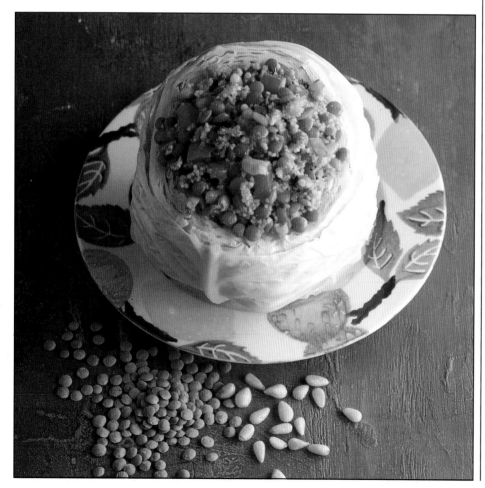

Couscous Aromatique 🌿

The cuisine of Morocco and Tunisia has many wonderful dishes using the wheat grain couscous which is steamed over simmering spicy stews. A little of the fiery harissa paste stirred in at the end adds an extra zing.

SERVES 4–6
450 g/1 lb couscous grains
60 ml/4 tbsp olive oil
1 onion, cut in chunks
2 carrots, cut in thick slices
4 baby turnips, halved
8 small new potatoes, halved
1 green pepper, cut in chunks
115 g/4 oz green beans, halved
1 small fennel bulb, sliced thickly
2.5 cm/1 in cube fresh root ginger, grated
2 garlic cloves, crushed
5 ml/1 tsp ground turmeric
15 ml/1 tbsp ground coriander
5 ml/1 tsp cumin seeds
5 ml/1 tsp ground cinnamon
45 ml/3 tbsp red lentils
1 × 400 g/14 oz can chopped tomatoes
1 litre/1¾ pints/4½ cups stock
60 ml/4 tbsp raisins
salt and ground black pepper
rind and juice of 1 lemon
harissa paste, to serve (optional)

1 Cover the couscous with cold water and soak for 10 minutes. Drain and spread out on a tray for 20 minutes, stirring it occasionally with your fingers.

2 Meanwhile, in a large saucepan, heat the oil and fry the vegetables for about 10 minutes, stirring from time to time.

3 Add the ginger, garlic and spices, stir well and cook for 2 minutes. Pour in the lentils, tomatoes, stock and raisins, and add seasoning.

4 Bring to a boil, then turn down to a simmer. By this time the couscous should be ready for steaming. Place in a steamer and fit this on top of the stew.

5 Cover and steam gently for about 20 minutes. The grains should be swollen and soft. Fork through and season well. Spoon into a serving dish.

6 Add the lemon rind and juice to the stew and check the seasoning. If liked, add harissa paste to taste; it is quite hot so beware! Serve the stew from a casserole dish separately. Spoon the couscous onto a plate and ladle the stew on top.

Cabbage Roulades with Lemon Sauce

Cabbage or chard leaves filled with a rice and lentil stuffing and served with a light eggy lemon sauce makes a light and tasty main course.

SERVES 4–6
12 large cabbage or chard leaves, stalks
   removed
salt
30 ml/2 tbsp sunflower oil
1 onion, chopped
1 large carrot, grated
115 g/4 oz sliced mushrooms
600 ml/1 pint/2½ cups stock
115 g/4 oz/½ cup long grain rice
60 ml/4 tbsp red lentils
5 ml/1 tsp dried oregano or marjoram
ground black pepper
100 g/3½ oz soft cheese with garlic
SAUCE
30 g/1 oz/3 tbsp plain flour
juice of 1 lemon
3 eggs, beaten

1 Blanch the leaves in boiling, salted water until they begin to wilt. Drain, reserve the water and pat the leaves dry with kitchen paper.

2 Heat the oil and lightly fry the onion, carrot and mushrooms for 5 minutes, and then pour in the stock.

3 Add the rice, lentils, herbs and seasoning. Bring to a boil, cover and simmer gently for 15 minutes. Remove, then stir in the cheese. Preheat the oven to 190°C/375°F/Gas 5.

4 Lay out the chard or cabbage leaves rib side down, and spoon on the filling at the stalk end. Fold the sides in and roll up.

5 Place the join side down in a small roasting pan and pour in the reserved cabbage water. Cover with lightly greased foil and bake for 30–45 minutes until the leaves are tender.

6 Remove the cabbage rolls from the oven, drain and place on a serving dish. Strain 600 ml/1 pint/2½ cups of the cooking water into a saucepan and bring to a boil.

7 Blend the flour to a runny paste with a little cold water and whisk into the boiling stock, together with the lemon juice.

8 Beat the eggs in a heatproof jug and slowly pour on the hot stock, whisking well as you go.

9 Return to the stove and on the lowest heat, stir until smooth and thick. Do not allow the sauce to boil or it will curdle. Serve the rolls with some of the sauce poured over and the rest handed separately.

Irish Colcannon

This lovely warming winter's dish bears a slight resemblance to Eggs Florentine. Here, baked eggs nestle among creamy potatoes with curly kale or cabbage and a topping of grated cheese.

SERVES 4

1 kg/2 lb potatoes, cut in even pieces
225 g/8 oz curly kale or crisp green
    cabbage, shredded
2 spring onions, chopped
butter or margarine, to taste
fresh nutmeg, grated
salt and ground black pepper
4 large eggs
75 g/3 oz mature cheese, grated

---

1 Boil the potatoes until just tender, then drain and mash well.

2 Lightly cook the kale or cabbage until just tender but still crisp. Preheat the oven to 190°C/375°F/Gas 5.

3 Drain the greens and mix them into the potato with the onions, butter or margarine and nutmeg. Season to taste.

4 Spoon the mixture into a shallow ovenproof dish and make four hollows in the mixture. Crack an egg into each and season well.

5 Bake for about 12 minutes or until the eggs are just set, then serve sprinkled with the cheese.

Pasta with Caponata

The Sicilians have an excellent sweet and sour vegetable dish called *caponata*, which naturally enough goes wonderfully well with pasta.

SERVES 4

1 medium aubergine, cut into sticks
2 medium courgettes, cut into sticks
8 baby onions, peeled or 1 large onion,
    sliced
2 garlic cloves, crushed
1 large red pepper, sliced
60 ml/4 tbsp olive oil, preferably extra
    virgin
450 ml/¾ pint/scant 2 cups tomato juice
    or 1 × 500 ml/17 fl oz carton creamed
    tomatoes
150 ml/¼ pint/⅔ cup water
30 ml/2 tbsp balsamic vinegar
juice of 1 lemon
15 ml/1 tbsp sugar
30 ml/2 tbsp sliced black olives
30 ml/2 tbsp capers
salt and ground black pepper
400 g/14 oz tagliatelle or other pasta
    ribbons

---

1 Lightly salt the aubergine and courgettes and leave them to drain in a colander for 30 minutes. Rinse and pat dry with kitchen paper towel.

2 In a large saucepan, lightly fry the onions, garlic and pepper in the oil for 5 minutes, then stir in the aubergine and courgettes and fry for a further 5 minutes.

3 Stir in the tomato juice or creamed tomatoes plus the water. Stir well, bringing the mixture to the boil, then add all the rest of the ingredients except the pasta. Season to taste and then simmer for 10 minutes.

4 Meanwhile, boil the pasta according to the instructions on the pack, then drain. Serve the caponata with the pasta.

Spinach Gnocchi

This wholesome Italian dish is ideal for making in advance then baking when required. Serve it with a fresh tomato sauce.

SERVES 4–6
400 g/14 oz fresh leaf spinach or 150 g/
  6 oz frozen leaf spinach, thawed
750 ml/1¼ pints/good 3 cups milk
200 g/7 oz/1¼ cups semolina
50 g/2 oz/4 tbsp butter, melted
50 g/2 oz Parmesan cheese, freshly
  grated, plus extra to serve
fresh nutmeg, grated
salt and ground black pepper
2 eggs, beaten

2 In a large saucepan, heat the milk and when just on the point of boiling, sprinkle in the semolina in a steady stream, stirring it briskly with a wooden spoon.

5 Stamp out shapes using a plain round cutter with a diameter of 4 cm/1½ in. Reserve the trimmings.

1 Blanch the spinach in the tiniest amount of water then drain and squeeze dry through a sieve with the back of a ladle. Chop the spinach roughly.

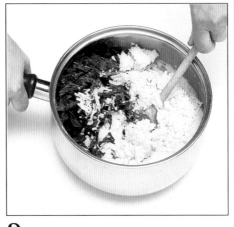

3 Simmer the semolina for 2 minutes then remove from the heat and stir in half the butter, most of the cheese, nutmeg and seasoning to taste and the spinach. Allow to cool for 5 minutes.

6 Grease a shallow ovenproof dish. Place the trimmings on the base and arrange the gnocchi rounds on top with each one overlapping.

7 Brush the tops with the remaining butter and sprinkle over the last of the cheese.

VARIATION

For a special occasion, make half plain and half spinach gnocchi and arrange in an attractive pattern to serve. Use the same recipe as above but halve the amount of spinach and add to half the mixture in a separate bowl to make two batches. Stamp out and cook the gnocchi as normal. For a more substantial, healthy meal, make a tasty vegetable base of lightly sautéed peppers, courgettes and mushrooms and place the gnocchi on the top.

4 Stir in the eggs then tip the mixture out onto a shallow baking sheet, spreading it to a 1 cm/½ in thickness. Allow to cool completely then chill until solid.

8 Preheat the oven when ready to bake to 190°C/375°F/Gas 5 and cook for about 35 minutes until golden and crisp on top. Serve hot with fresh tomato sauce and extra cheese.

Red Rice Rissoles

Risotto rice chills to a firm texture yet remains light and creamy when reheated as crisp crumbed rissoles. These contain small nuggets of cheese for extra creaminess.

SERVES ABOUT 8
1 large red onion, chopped
1 red pepper, chopped
2 garlic cloves, crushed
1 red chilli, finely chopped
30 ml/2 tbsp olive oil
25 g/1 oz/2 tbsp butter
225 g/8 oz/1¼ cups risotto rice
1 litre/1¾ pints/4½ cups stock
4 sun-dried tomatoes, chopped
30 ml/2 tbsp tomato purée
10 ml/2 tsp dried oregano
salt and ground black pepper
45 ml/3 tbsp fresh parsley, chopped
150 g/6 oz cheese, e.g. Red Leicester or
　smoked Cheddar
1 egg, beaten
115 g/4 oz/1 cup dried breadcrumbs
oil, for deep frying

1 Fry the onion, pepper, garlic and chilli in the oil and butter for 5 minutes. Stir in the rice and fry for a further 2 minutes.

2 Pour in the stock and add the tomatoes, purée, oregano and seasoning. Bring to the boil, stirring occasionally, then cover and simmer for 20 minutes.

3 Stir in the parsley then turn into a shallow dish, cool and chill until firm. When cold, divide into 12 and shape into balls.

4 Cut the cheese into 12 pieces and press a nugget into the centre of each of the rissoles.

5 Put the beaten egg in one bowl and the breadcrumbs into another. Dip the rissoles first into the egg then into the breadcrumbs, coating each one evenly.

6 Lay the coated rissoles on a plate and chill again for 30 minutes. Fill a deep fat frying pan one-third full of oil and heat until a cube of day-old bread browns in under a minute.

7 Fry the rissoles in batches, reheating the oil in between, for about 3–4 minutes. Drain on kitchen paper and keep warm, uncovered, before serving.

Broad Bean and Cauliflower Curry

A tasty mid-week curry to serve with rice (especially a brown basmati), small popadums and maybe a cucumber raita.

SERVES 4
2 garlic cloves, chopped
2.5 cm/1 in cube fresh root ginger
1 fresh green chilli, seeded and chopped
15 ml/1 tbsp oil
1 onion, sliced
1 large potato, chopped
30 ml/2 tbsp ghee or softened butter
15 ml/1 tbsp curry powder, mild or hot
1 medium size cauliflower, cut into small
  florets
600 ml/1 pint/2½ cups stock
25 g/1 oz/2 tbsp creamed coconut
salt and ground black pepper
1 × 285 g/10 oz can broad beans, with
  liquor
juice of half a lemon (optional)
fresh coriander or parsley, chopped,
  to serve

1 Blend the garlic, ginger, chilli and oil in a food processor until they form a smooth paste.

2 In a large saucepan, fry the onion and potato in the ghee or butter for 5 minutes then stir in the spice paste and curry powder. Cook for 1 minute.

3 Add the cauliflower florets and stir well into the spicy mixture, then pour in the stock. Bring to a boil and mix in the coconut, stirring until it melts.

4 Season well then cover and simmer for 10 minutes. Add the beans and their liquor and cook uncovered for a further 10 minutes.

5 Check the seasoning and add a good squeeze of lemon juice if liked. Serve hot garnished with coriander or parsley.

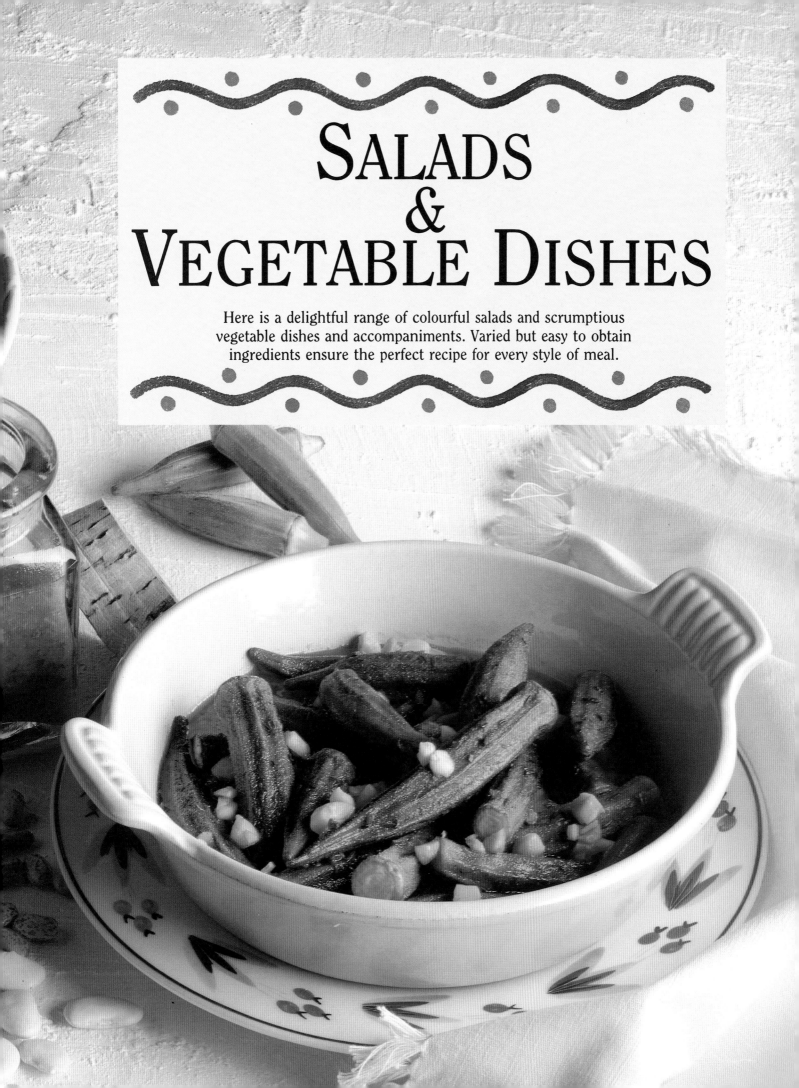

SALADS & VEGETABLE DISHES

Here is a delightful range of colourful salads and scrumptious vegetable dishes and accompaniments. Varied but easy to obtain ingredients ensure the perfect recipe for every style of meal.

Bean Sprout Stir-fry

Homegrown bean sprouts taste so good, tossed into a tasty stir-fry. They have more flavour and texture than shop bought varieties and are very nutritious, being rich in vitamins and high in fibre. (Old dried beans will not sprout, so use beans that are well within their 'Use by' date.)

SERVES 3–4
30 ml/2 tbsp sunflower or groundnut oil
225 g/8 oz mixed sprouted beans
2 spring onions, chopped
1 garlic clove, crushed
30 ml/2 tbsp soy sauce
10 ml/2 tsp sesame oil
15 ml/1 tbsp sesame seeds
30 ml/2 tbsp fresh coriander or parsley, chopped
salt and ground black pepper

1 Heat the sunflower or groundnut oil in a large wok and stir-fry the sprouting beans, onion and garlic for 3–5 minutes.

2 Add the remaining ingredients, cook for 1–2 minutes more and serve hot.

HOME SPROUTING BEANS

Use any of the following pulses to grow your own sprouts: green or brown lentils, aduki beans, mung beans, chick peas, flageolet and haricot beans, soya beans or Indian massor dal.

Cover 45 ml/3 tbsp of your chosen pulses with lukewarm water. Leave to soak overnight, then drain and rinse.

Place in a large clean jam jar or special sprouting tray. Cover with muslin and secure with a rubber band. If using a jam jar, lay the jar on its side and shake it so the beans spread along the length. Leave somewhere warm.

Rinse the beans night and morning with plenty of cold water, running this through the muslin, and drain. Carefully place the jar back on its side.

Repeat this twice a day until roots and shoots appear. (If nothing happens after 48 hours, the beans are probably too old.) When the shoots are at least twice the length of the bean, rinse finally and store in the fridge for up to two days.

Panzanella Salad

If sliced juicy tomatoes layered with day old bread sounds strange for a salad, don't be deceived – it's quite delicious. A popular Italian salad, this dish is ideal as a starter or an accompaniment. Use full-flavoured tomatoes for the best result.

SERVES 4–6
4 thick slices day-old bread, either white, brown or rye
1 small red onion, thinly sliced
450 g/1 lb ripe tomatoes, thinly sliced
115 g/4 oz Mozzarella cheese, thinly sliced
5 ml/1 tbsp fresh basil, shredded, or marjoram
salt and ground black pepper
120 ml/4 fl oz/½ cup extra virgin olive oil
45 ml/3 tbsp balsamic vinegar
juice of 1 small lemon
stoned and sliced black olives or salted capers, to garnish

1 Dip the bread briefly in cold water, then carefully squeeze out the excess water. Arrange on the bottom of a shallow salad bowl.

2 Soak the onion slices in cold water for about 10 minutes while you prepare the other ingredients. Drain and reserve.

3 Layer the tomatoes, cheese, onion, basil or marjoram, seasoning well in between each layer. Sprinkle with oil, vinegar and lemon juice.

4 Top with the olives or capers, cover with cling film and chill in the refrigerator overnight, if possible.

Caesar's Salad

On Independence Day 1924, in Tijuana, Mexico, a restaurateur – Caesar Cardini – created this masterpiece of new American cuisine. It has all the elements of a good salad – being light, flavoursome, attractive and nutritious with a good crunch.

SERVES 4
2 thick slices crustless bread
2 garlic cloves
sunflower oil, for frying
1 Cos lettuce, torn in pieces
50 g/2 oz/½ cup fresh Parmesan cheese, coarsely grated
2 eggs

DRESSING
30 ml/2 tbsp extra virgin olive oil
10 ml/2 tsp French mustard
10 ml/2 tsp Worcestershire sauce
30 ml/2 tbsp fresh lemon juice

1   Cut the bread into cubes. Heat one of the garlic cloves slowly in about 45 ml/3 tbsp of the sunflower oil in a saucepan then toss in the bread cubes. Remove the garlic clove.

2   Heat an oven to 190°C/375°F/Gas 5. Spread the garlicky cubes on a baking sheet and bake the bread for about 10–12 minutes until golden and crisp. Remove and allow to cool.

3   Rub the inside of a large salad bowl with the remaining garlic clove and then discard it.

4   Toss in the torn lettuce, sprinkling between the leaves with the cheese. Cover and set the salad aside.

5   Boil a small saucepan of water and cook the eggs for 1 minute only. Remove the eggs, and crack them open into a jug or bowl. The whites should be milky and the yolks raw.

6   Whisk the dressing ingredients into the eggs. When ready to serve pour the dressing over the leaves, toss well together and serve topped with the croûtons.

VARIATION

Why not try a refreshing Italian version of this salad? Use cubed ciabatta bread for the croûtons. Rub the inside of a salad bowl with garlic and spoon in 30–45 ml/2–3 tbsp of good olive oil. Add a selection of torn salad leaves, including rocket, together with some shaved Parmesan cheese. Do not mix yet. Just before serving, add the croûtons, season well, then toss the leaves with the oil, coating well. Finally squeeze over the juice of a fresh lemon.

Chef's Salad

This is basically whatever you make of it – a lovely large salad containing all your favourite ingredients. It is also a good opportunity to use up leftover vegetables and small pieces of cheese from the refrigerator. For these reasons, quantities are approximate.

SERVES 6
450 g/1 lb new potatoes, halved if large
2 carrots, grated coarsely
½ small fennel bulb or 2 sticks celery, sliced thinly
50 g/2 oz sliced button mushrooms
¼ cucumber, sliced or chopped
small green or red pepper, sliced
60 ml/4 tbsp garden peas
200 g/7 oz/1 cup cooked pulses, e.g. red kidney beans or green lentils
1 Ice Gem or baby lettuce or 1 head chicory (endive)
2–3 hard boiled eggs, quartered and/or grated cheese, to serve
½ carton salad cress, snipped

DRESSING
60 ml/4 tbsp mayonnaise
45 ml/3 tbsp natural yogurt
30 ml/2 tbsp milk
30 ml/2 tbsp chopped fresh chives or spring onion tops
salt and ground black pepper

1 Put all the vegetables and pulses (except the lettuce or chicory) into a large mixing bowl.

2 Line a large platter with the lettuce or chicory leaves – creating a nest for the other salad ingredients. Mix the dressing ingredients together and pour over the salad in the mixing bowl.

3 Toss the salad thoroughly in the dressing, season well then pile into the centre of the lettuce nest.

4 Top the salad with the eggs, cheese or both and sprinkle with the snipped cress. Serve lightly chilled.

Potato and Radish Salad

So many potato salads are dressed in thick sauce. This one is quite light and colourful with a flavoursome yet delicate dressing.

SERVES 4–6
450 g/1 lb new potatoes, scrubbed
45 ml/3 tbsp olive oil
15 ml/1 tbsp walnut or hazelnut oil
 (optional)
30 ml/2 tbsp wine vinegar
10 ml/2 tsp coarse grain mustard
5 ml/1 tsp clear honey
salt and ground black pepper
about 6–8 radishes, thinly sliced
30 ml/2 tbsp fresh chives, chopped

1 Boil the potatoes until just tender. Drain, return to the pan and cut any large potatoes in half.

2 Make a dressing with the oils, vinegar, mustard, honey and seasoning. Mix them together thoroughly in a bowl.

3 Toss the dressing into the potatoes while they are still cooling and allow them to stand for an hour or so.

4 Mix in the radishes and chives, chill lightly, toss again and serve.

COOK'S TIP

The secret of a good potato salad is to dress the potatoes while still warm in a vinaigrette-style dressing in order to let them soak up the flavour as they cool. You can then mix in an additional creamy dressing of mayonnaise and natural yogurt if liked. Sliced celery, red onion and chopped walnuts would make a good alternative to the radishes and, for best effect, serve on a platter lined with frilly lettuce leaves.

Thai Rice and Sprouting Beans

Thai rice has a delicate fragrance and texture that is delicious whether served hot or cold. This salad is a colourful collection of popular Thai flavours and textures.

SERVES 6
30 ml/2 tbsp sesame oil
30 ml/2 tbsp fresh lime juice
1 small fresh red chilli, seeded and chopped
1 garlic clove, crushed
10 ml/2 tsp grated fresh root ginger
30 ml/2 tbsp light soy sauce
5 ml/1 tsp clear honey
45 ml/3 tbsp pineapple juice
15 ml/1 tbsp wine vinegar
225 g/8 oz/1¼ cups Thai fragrant rice, boiled
2 spring onions, sliced
2 rings canned pineapple in natural juice, chopped
150 g/5 oz/1¼ cups sprouted lentils or bean sprouts
1 small red pepper, sliced
1 stick celery, sliced
50 g/2 oz/½ cup unsalted cashew nuts, roughly chopped
30 ml/2 tbsp toasted sesame seeds
salt and ground black pepper

1 Whisk together the sesame oil, lime juice, chilli, garlic, ginger, soy sauce, honey, pineapple juice and vinegar in a large bowl. Stir in the lightly boiled rice.

2 Toss in all the remaining ingredients and mix well. This dish can be served warm or lightly chilled. If the rice grains stick together on cooling, simply stir them with a metal spoon.

Chicory, Carrot and Rocket Salad

A bright and colourful salad which is ideal for a buffet or barbecue party. Use watercress if you are unable to obtain any rocket.

SERVES 4–6
3 carrots, coarsely grated
about 50 g/2 oz fresh rocket or watercress, roughly chopped
1 large head chicory
DRESSING:
45 ml/3 tbsp sunflower oil
15 ml/1 tbsp hazelnut or walnut oil (optional)
30 ml/2 tbsp cider or wine vinegar
10 ml/2 tsp clear honey
5 ml/1 tsp grated lemon rind
15 ml/1 tbsp poppy seeds
salt and ground black pepper

1 Mix the carrot and rocket or watercress together in a large bowl and season well.

2 Shake the dressing ingredients together in a screw-topped jar then pour onto the carrot and greenery. Toss the salad thoroughly.

3 Line a shallow salad bowl with the chicory leaves and spoon the salad into the centre. Serve lightly chilled.

Bountiful Bean and Nut Salad 🥬

This is a good multi-purpose dish. It can be a cold main course, a buffet party dish, or a salad on the side. It also keeps well for up to three days in the refrigerator.

SERVES 6

75 g/3 oz/½ cup red kidney, pinto or
  borlotti beans
75 g/3 oz/½ cup white cannellini or butter
  beans
30 ml/2 tbsp olive oil
175 g/6 oz cut fresh green beans
3 spring onions, sliced
1 small yellow or red pepper, sliced
1 carrot, coarsely grated
30 ml/2 tbsp dried topping onions or
  sun-dried tomatoes, chopped
50 g/2 oz/½ cup unsalted cashew nuts or
  almonds, split

DRESSING

45 ml/3 tbsp sunflower oil
30 ml/2 tbsp red wine vinegar
15 ml/1 tbsp coarse grain mustard
5 ml/1 tsp caster sugar
5 ml/1 tsp dried mixed herbs
salt and ground black pepper

1 Soak the beans, overnight if possible, then drain and rinse well, cover with a lot of cold water and cook according to the instructions on the pack.

2 When cooked, drain and season the beans and toss them in the olive oil. Leave to cool for 30 minutes.

3 In a large bowl, mix in the other vegetables, including the sun-dried tomatoes but not the crisp topping onions, if using, or the nuts.

4 Make up the dressing by shaking all the ingredients together in a screw topped jar. Toss the dressing into the salad and check the seasoning again. Serve sprinkled with the topping onions, if using, and the split nuts.

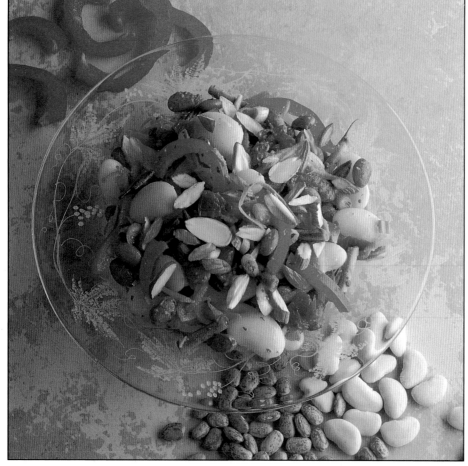

Garden Salad and Garlic Crostini

Dress a colourful mixture of salad leaves with good olive oil and freshly squeezed lemon juice, then top it with crispy bread crostini.

SERVES 4–6
3 thick slices day old bread, e.g. ciabatta
120 ml/4 fl oz/½ cup extra virgin olive oil
garlic clove, cut
½ small Cos or Romaine lettuce
½ small oak leaf lettuce
25 g/1 oz rocket leaves or cress
25 g/1 oz fresh flat leaf parsley
a few leaves and flowers of nasturtium
flowers of pansy and pot marigold
a small handful of young dandelion
   leaves
sea salt flakes and ground black pepper
juice of 1 fresh lemon

1 Cut the bread into medium size dice about 1 cm/½ in square.

2 Heat half the oil gently in a frying pan and fry the bread cubes in it, tossing them until they are well coated and lightly browned. Remove and cool.

3 Rub the inside of a large salad bowl with the garlic and discard. Pour the rest of the oil into the bottom of the bowl.

4 Wash, dry and tear the leaves into bite size pieces and pile them into the bowl. Season with salt and pepper. Cover and keep chilled until ready to serve.

5 To serve, toss the leaves in the oil at the bottom of the bowl, then sprinkle with the lemon juice and toss again. Scatter over the crostini and serve immediately.

Californian Vim and Vit Salad 🍃

Full of vitality and vitamins, this is a lovely light healthy salad for sunny days when you feel full of energy, or need an extra boost.

SERVES 4
1 small crisp lettuce, torn in pieces
225 g/8 oz young spinach leaves
2 carrots, coarsely grated
115 g/4 oz cherry tomatoes, halved
2 celery sticks, thinly sliced
75 g/3 oz/½ cup raisins
50 g/2 oz/½ cup blanched almonds or
   unsalted cashew nuts, halved
30 ml/2 tbsp sunflower seeds
30 ml/2 tbsp sesame seeds, lightly toasted
DRESSING:
45 ml/3 tbsp extra virgin olive oil
30 ml/2 tbsp cider vinegar
10 ml/2 tsp clear honey
juice of 1 small orange
salt and ground black pepper

1 Put the salad vegetables, raisins, almonds or cashew nuts and seeds into a large bowl.

2 Put all the dressing ingredients into a screw top jar, shake them up well and pour over the salad.

3 Toss the salad thoroughly and divide it between four small salad bowls. Season and serve lightly chilled.

Scandinavian Cucumber and Dill

It's amazing what a touch of salt can do to simple cucumber slices. They take on a contradictory soft yet crisp texture and develop a good, full flavour. However, juices continue to form after salting, so this salad is best dressed just before serving. It is particularly complementary to hot and spicy food.

SERVES 4
2 cucumbers
salt
30 ml/2 tbsp fresh chives, chopped
30 ml/2 tbsp fresh dill, chopped
150 ml/¼ pint/⅔ cup soured cream or
   fromage frais
ground black pepper

1 Slice the cucumbers as thinly as possible, preferably in a food processor or a slicer.

2 Place the slices in layers in a colander set over a plate to catch the juices. Sprinkling each layer well, but not too heavily, with salt.

3 Leave the cucumber to drain for up to 2 hours, then lay out the slices on a clean tea towel and pat them dry.

4 Mix the cucumber with the herbs, cream or fromage frais and plenty of pepper. Serve as soon as possible.

COOK'S TIP

Lightly salted (or degorged) cucumbers are also delicious as sandwich fillings in wafer thin buttered brown bread. These sandwiches were always served at the traditional British tea-time.

Useful Dressings

A good dressing can make even the simplest combination of fresh vegetables a memorable treat. Remember, in addition to normal salads, lightly cooked hot vegetables such as carrots and potatoes or pulses and grains absorb more flavour and are less greasy if dressed while hot.

Homemade Mayonnaise

Make this by hand, if possible. If you make it in a food processor, it will be noticeably lighter.

---

2 egg yolks
2.5 ml/½ tsp salt
2.5 ml/½ tsp dry mustard
ground black pepper
300 ml/½ pint/1¼ cups sunflower oil or half olive and half sunflower oil
15 ml/1 tbsp wine vinegar
15 ml/1 tbsp hot water

---

1 Put the yolks into a bowl with the salt and mustard and a grinding of pepper.

2 Stand the bowl on a damp dish cloth. Using a whisk, beat the yolks and the seasoning thoroughly, then beat in a small trickle of oil.

3 Continue trickling in the oil, adding it in very small amounts. The secret of a good, thick mayonnaise is to add the oil very slowly, beating each addition well before you add more. When all the oil is added, mix in the vinegar and hot water.

To make mayonnaise in a blender, use one whole egg and one yolk instead of two yolks. Blend the eggs with the seasonings. Then, with the blades running, trickle in the oil very slowly. Add the vinegar.

Original Thousand Islands Dressing

---

60 ml/4 tbsp sunflower oil
15 ml/1 tbsp fresh orange juice
15 ml/1 tbsp fresh lemon juice
10 ml/2 tsp grated lemon rind
15 ml/1 tbsp finely chopped onion
5 ml/1 tsp paprika
5 ml/1 tsp Worcestershire sauce
15 ml/1 tbsp finely chopped parsley
salt and ground black pepper

Put all the ingredients into a screw-topped jar, season to taste and shake vigorously. Great with green salads, grated carrot, hot potato, pasta and rice salads.

Yogurt Dressing

---

150 g/5 oz/⅔ cup natural yogurt
30 ml/2 tbsp mayonnaise
30 ml/2 tbsp milk
15 ml/1 tbsp fresh parsley, chopped
15 ml/1 tbsp fresh chives or spring onions, chopped
salt and ground black pepper

Simply mix all the ingredients together thoroughly in a bowl.

Peperonata with Raisins

Sliced roasted peppers in dressing with vinegar-soaked raisins make a tasty side salad which complements many other dishes and is quick to make, especially if you already have a batch of peppers in oil.

SERVES 2–4

90 ml/6 tbsp sliced peppers in olive oil, drained
15 ml/1 tbsp onion, chopped
30 ml/2 tbsp balsamic vinegar
45 ml/3 tbsp raisins
30 ml/2 tbsp fresh parsley, chopped
ground black pepper

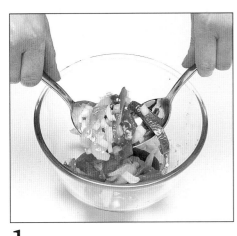

1 Toss the peppers with the onion and leave to steep for an hour.

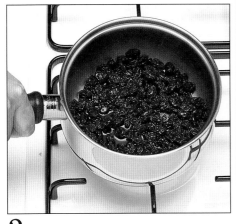

2 Put the vinegar and raisins in a small saucepan and heat for a minute, then allow to cool.

3 Mix all the ingredients together thoroughly and spoon into a serving bowl. Serve lightly chilled.

COOK'S TIP

Peperonata is one of the classic Italian antipasto dishes, served at the start of each meal with crusty bread to mop up the delicious juices. Try serving shavings of fresh Parmesan cheese alongside, or buy a good selection of green and black olives to accompany the peperonata. Small baby tomatoes will complete the antipasto.

Spinach Roulade

A simple purée of spinach baked with eggs rolled around a creamy red pepper filling makes an exotic and colourful side dish. Even better, this can be prepared in advance and then reheated when required.

SERVES 4
450 g/1 lb leaf spinach, well washed and drained
fresh nutmeg, grated
good knob of butter
45 ml/3 tbsp Parmesan cheese, grated
45 ml/3 tbsp double cream
salt and ground black pepper
2 eggs, separated
1 small red pepper, chopped
1 × 200 g/7 oz pack soft cheese with garlic and herbs

1 Line and then grease a medium-sized Swiss roll tin. Preheat the oven to 190°C/375°F/Gas 5.

2 Cook the spinach with a tiny amount of water then drain well, pressing it through a sieve with the back of a ladle. Chop the spinach finely.

3 Mix the spinach with the nutmeg, butter, Parmesan cheese, cream and seasoning. Cool for 5 minutes then beat in the egg yolks.

4 Whisk the egg whites until they form soft peaks and carefully fold in to the spinach mixture. Spread in to the prepared tin, level and bake for 12–15 minutes until firm.

5 Turn the spinach out upside down on to a clean tea towel and allow it to cool in the tin for half an hour.

6 Meanwhile, simmer the pepper in about 30 ml/2 tbsp of water in a covered pan until just soft, then either purée it in a blender or chop it finely. Mix with the soft cheese and season well.

7 When the spinach has cooled, peel off the paper. Trim any hard edges and spread it with the red pepper cream.

8 Carefully roll up the spinach and pepper in the tea towel, leave for 10 minutes to firm up, then serve on a long platter, cut in thick slices.

VARIATION

A thick vegetable purée of any root vegetable also works well as a roulade. Try cooked beetroot or parsnip, flavouring lightly with a mild curry-style spice such as cumin or coriander. The fillings can be varied too, such as finely chopped and sautéed mushroom and onion or grated carrot mixed with fromage frais and chives. Roulades are delicious served warm as well. Sprinkle with cheese and bake in a moderately hot oven for 15 minutes or so.

Mighty Mushrooms

There is now a wide variety of cultivated mushrooms on sale in larger supermarkets and greengrocers so a simple side dish of mushrooms becomes quite exciting. This also makes an excellent sauce to serve tossed into pasta. Dried ceps or porcini mushrooms are on sale in delicatessens if you have trouble finding them in supermarkets.

SERVES 4

15 g/½ oz pack dried porcini mushrooms/ceps (optional)
60 ml/4 tbsp olive oil
225 g/8 oz button mushrooms, halved or sliced
115 g/4 oz oyster mushrooms
115 g/4 oz fresh shiitake mushrooms, or 25 g/1 oz dried and soaked mushrooms
2 garlic cloves, crushed
10 ml/2 tsp ground coriander
salt and ground black pepper
45 ml/3 tbsp fresh parsley, chopped

1 If you are using porcini mushrooms (and they do give a good rich flavour), soak them in a little hot water just to cover for 20 minutes.

2 In a large saucepan, heat the oil and add all the mushrooms, including the soaked porcinis, if using. Stir well, cover and cook gently for 5 minutes.

3 Stir in the garlic, coriander and seasoning. Cook for another 5 minutes until the mushrooms are tender and much of the liquor has been reduced.

4 Mix in the parsley, allow to cool slightly and serve.

Tomato Sauce

A basic sauce which can either be part of a larger recipe or served as a side sauce. For extra flavour, add red pepper, or ring the changes with orange rind and juice, chopped fresh herbs such as basil, or spice it up with chilli sauce.

SERVES 4–6

1 onion, chopped
2 garlic cloves, crushed
1 small red pepper (optional), chopped
45 ml/3 tbsp olive oil
675 g/1½ lb fresh tomatoes, skinned and chopped or 1 × 400 g/14 oz can chopped tomatoes
15 g/½ oz granulated sugar
salt and ground black pepper
30 ml/2 tbsp fresh herbs, chopped, e.g. basil, parsley, marjoram (optional)

1 Gently fry the onion, garlic and red pepper, if using, in the oil for 5 minutes until they are soft.

2 Stir in the tomatoes, add the sugar and seasoning to taste, bring to a boil then cover and simmer for 15–20 minutes.

3 The sauce should now be thick and pulpy. If it is a little thin, then boil it – uncovered – so that it reduces down. Stir in the fresh herbs, if using, and then check the seasoning.

COOK'S TIP

Why not make up a large batch of this sauce and freeze it in two-portion sizes?

Indian Spiced Okra with Almonds

Long and elegantly shaped, it's not surprising these vegetables have the popular name of 'lady's fingers'. Although commonly used in many international dishes, okra are particularly well suited to all the Indian spices.

SERVES 2—4
225 g/8 oz okra
50 g/2 oz/½ cup blanched almonds, chopped
25 g/1 oz/2 tbsp butter
15 ml/1 tbsp sunflower oil
2 garlic cloves, crushed
2.5 cm/1 in cube fresh root ginger, grated
5 ml/1 tsp cumin seeds
5 ml/1 tsp ground coriander
5 ml/1 tsp paprika

1 Trim just the tops of the okra stems and around the edges of the stalks. They have a sticky liquid which oozes out if prepared too far ahead, so trim them immediately before cooking.

2 In a shallow fireproof dish, fry the almonds in the butter until they are lightly golden, then remove.

3 Add the oil to the pan and fry the okra, stirring constantly, for 2 minutes.

4 Add the garlic and ginger and fry gently for a minute, then add the spices and cook for another minute or so, stirring all the time.

VARIATION

Okra are also popular in Louisiana cooking and are an essential ingredient for gumbo, a thick, spicy stew served over hot, steaming rice. Indeed, 'gumbo' was the old African word for okra used by the American slaves. You can make a ratatouille-style vegetable stew using okra instead of aubergines, and adding onions, peppers, garlic and tomatoes. Or try them sliced, fried in garlic and spices, then stirred into a pilaff of basmati rice with cauliflower florets and carrots. This makes a colourful and delicious dish – especially when topped with crushed grilled popadums.

5 Pour in about 300 ml/½ pint/1¼ cups water. Season well, cover and simmer for about 5 minutes or so until the okra feel just tender.

6 Finally, mix in the fried almonds and serve piping hot.

Stir-fry Cabbage

An often under-rated vegetable, crisp cabbage is wonderful when lightly cooked the Chinese way in a wok. Any cabbage will do, but perhaps the Savoy cabbage is the nicest.

SERVES 4
½ small cabbage
30 ml/2 tbsp sunflower oil
15 ml/1 tbsp light soy sauce
15 ml/1 tbsp fresh lemon juice (optional)
10 ml/2 tsp caraway seeds
ground black pepper

1 Cut the central core from the cabbage, and shred the leaves finely.

2 Heat the oil until quite hot in a wok and then stir-fry the cabbage for about 2 minutes.

3 Toss in the soy sauce, lemon juice, if using, caraway seeds and pepper, to taste.

Perfect Creamed Potatoes

If a bowl of plain, mashed potatoes sounds boring, then try serving it this way – in the French style. It is absolutely scrumptious!

SERVES 4
1 kg/2 lb potatoes, peeled and diced
45 ml/3 tbsp extra virgin olive oil
about 150 ml/¼ pint/⅔ cup milk
fresh nutmeg, grated
salt and ground black pepper
a few leaves fresh basil or sprigs fresh
  parsley, chopped

COOK'S TIP

Choosing the right potato makes all the difference to creamed or mashed potatoes. A waxy variety won't be light and fluffy, and a potato which breaks down too quickly on boiling will become a slurry when mashed. Most bags of potatoes carry guidelines on what method of cooking they are suited for. In general, red potatoes make a good mash, as do Maris Piper and King Edwards.

1 Boil the potatoes until just tender and not too mushy. Drain very well. Ideally press the potatoes through a special potato 'ricer' (rather like a large garlic press) or mash them well with a potato masher. Do not pass them through a food processor or you will have a gluey mess.

2 Beat the olive oil into the potato and just enough hot milk to make a smooth, thick purée.

3 Flavour to taste with the nutmeg and seasoning then stir in the fresh chopped herbs. Spoon into a warm serving dish and serve as soon as possible.

Roasted Peppers in Oil

Peppers take on a delicious, smoky flavour if roasted in a very hot oven. The skins can easily be peeled off and the flesh stored in olive oil. This oil can then be used to add extra flavour to salad dressings.

6 large peppers of differing colours
450 ml/¾ pint/scant 2 cups olive oil

1 Preheat the oven to the highest temperature, about 230°C/450°F/Gas 8. Lightly grease a large baking sheet.

2 Quarter the peppers, remove the cores and seeds then squash them flat with the back of your hands. Lay the peppers skin side up on the baking tray.

3 Roast the peppers at the top of the oven until the skins blacken and blister. This will take about 12–15 minutes.

4 Remove the peppers from the oven, cover with a clean tea towel until they are cool, then peel off the skins.

5 Slice the peppers and pack them into a clean preserving jar.

6 Add the oil to the jar to completely cover the peppers, then seal the lid tightly.

7 Store the peppers in the refrigerator and use them within 2 weeks. Use the oil in dressing or for cooking once the peppers have been eaten.

COOK'S TIP

These pepper slices make very attractive presents, especially around Christmas time. You can either buy special preserving jars from kitchen equipment shops, or wash out large jam jars, soaking off the labels at the same time. The jars should then be sterilized by placing upside down in a low oven for about half an hour. Fill the jars while still hot with the sliced peppers, and fill with a good olive oil. Cover immediately with the lid and fix on an attractive label.

Oven Chip Roasties

Very popular with children and a much better alternative for all the family to high fat roast potatoes.

SERVES 4–6
4 medium to large baking potatoes
150 ml/¼ pint/⅔ cup olive oil
5 ml/1 tsp dried mixed herbs (optional)
sea salt flakes

1 Preheat the oven to the highest possible temperature, generally 230°C/450°F/Gas 8. Place a lightly-oiled roasting tin in the oven to get really hot.

2 Cut the potatoes in half lengthways then into long thin wedges. Brush each side lightly with oil.

3 When the oven is really hot, remove the pan carefully and scatter the potato slices over it in a single layer.

4 Sprinkle the potatoes with the herbs and salt and place in the oven for about 20 minutes or until they are golden brown, crisp and lightly puffy. Serve immediately.

VARIATION

Parsnips also make fine oven chips. Choose large parsnips which tend to have more flavour. Slice thinly on a diagonal and roast in the same way as above, although you may find they do not take as long to cook. They make great mid-week suppers for kids and grown-ups served with fried eggs, mushrooms and tomatoes.

Warm Spicy Dhal

If you thought split yellow peas were only for soups, then try this Indian inspired dish. Serve with rice, chappatis or naan bread and whatever main dish you like. Try eggs, fried aubergines, or even a tasty dish of fried mushrooms.

SERVES 4–6
225 g/8 oz yellow split peas
2 onions, chopped
1 large bay leaf
600 ml/1 pint/2½ cups stock or water
salt and ground black pepper
10 ml/2 tsp black mustard seeds
30 ml/2 tbsp melted butter
1 garlic clove, crushed
2.5 cm/1 in cube fresh root ginger, grated
1 small green pepper, sliced
5 ml/1 tsp ground turmeric
5 ml/1 tsp garam masala or mild curry powder
3 tomatoes, skinned and chopped
fresh coriander or parsley, to serve

1 Put the split peas, 1 onion and the bay leaf in the stock or water, in a covered pan. Simmer for 25 minutes, seasoning lightly towards the end.

2 In a separate pan, fry the mustard seeds in the butter for about 30 seconds until they start to pop, then add all the remaining onion, along with the garlic, ginger and green pepper.

3 Sauté for about 5 minutes until softened then stir in the remaining spices and fry for a few seconds more.

4 Add the split peas, tomatoes, and a little extra water if it needs it. Cover and simmer for a further 10 minutes, then check the seasoning and serve hot garnished with coriander or parsley.

Potato Latkes

These little potato pancakes make a pleasant and unusual alternative to chips or roast potatoes.

MAKES ABOUT 24
1 kg/2 lb potatoes, peeled and coarsely grated
40 g/1½ oz/scant ½ cup self-raising flour
2 eggs
15 ml/1 tbsp onion, grated
fresh nutmeg, grated
salt and ground black pepper
oil, for shallow frying

1 Soak the grated potato in plenty of cold water for about an hour, then drain well and pat dry with a clean tea towel.

2 Beat together the flour, eggs, onion and nutmeg, then mix in the potato. Season well.

3 Heat a thin layer of oil in a heavy based frying pan and drop about a tablespoon of potato batter into the pan, squashing it flat, if necessary.

4 Cook the potato until golden brown, then flip over and cook the other side. Drain on kitchen paper towel and keep warm, uncovered in the oven. Repeat with the rest of the mixture.

Stir-fry Aubergine

A speedy side dish with an Oriental touch. The aubergine is stir-fried with red pepper and black beans which gives it an exotic and colourful appearance. Salted black beans are sold either dried or canned. Dried ones will need soaking.

SERVES 4
30 ml/2 tbsp groundnut oil
1 aubergine, sliced
2 spring onions, sliced diagonally
1 garlic clove, crushed
1 small red pepper, sliced
30 ml/2 tbsp oyster sauce
25 g/1 oz/1 tbsp Chinese salted black beans, soaked if dried
ground black pepper
15 ml/1 tbsp fresh coriander or parsley, chopped, to garnish

1 Heat the oil in a wok and stir-fry the aubergine for 2 minutes. Add the onions, garlic and pepper and cook for a further 2 minutes.

2 Add the oyster sauce, black beans and pepper. Cook for a further 1 minute, season with pepper only and serve with fresh coriander or parsley.

Peas and Lettuce

Do not discard the tough, outer leaves of lettuce – they are delicious if shredded and cooked with peas.

SERVES 4
6 outer leaves of lettuce, e.g. Cos, Webbs
1 small onion or shallot, sliced
25 g/1 oz/2 tbsp butter or sunflower margarine
225 g/8 oz frozen garden peas
fresh nutmeg, grated
salt and ground black pepper

1 Pull off the outer lettuce leaves and wash them well. Roughly shred the leaves with your hands.

2 In a saucepan, lightly fry the lettuce and onion or shallot in the butter or margarine for 3 minutes.

3 Add the peas, nutmeg to taste and seasoning. Stir, cover and simmer for about 5 minutes. This dish can be drained or served slightly wet.

Hash Browns

A traditional American breakfast dish, hash browns can be served any time of day. They are a tasty way of using up any left over boiled potatoes.

SERVES 4
60 ml/4 tbsp sunflower or olive oil
about 450 g/1 lb diced, cooked potatoes
1 small onion, chopped
salt and ground black pepper

1 Heat the oil in a large, heavy-based frying pan and when quite hot add the potatoes in a single layer. Scatter the onion on top and season well.

2 Cook on a moderate heat until browned underneath, pressing down on the potatoes with a spoon or spatula to squash them together.

3 When the potatoes are nicely browned, turn them over in sections with a fish slice and fry on the other side, pressing them down once again. Serve when heated through and lightly crispy.

Potato and Parsnip Dauphinoise

Layers of potatoes and parsnips are baked slowly in creamy milk with grated cheese. This is an ideal special side dish or light supper dish.

SERVES 4–6
1 kg/2 lb potatoes, thinly sliced
1 onion, thinly sliced
450 g/1 lb parsnips, thinly sliced
2 garlic cloves, crushed
50 g/2 oz/4 tbsp butter
125 g/4 oz Gruyère or Cheddar cheese, grated
fresh nutmeg, grated
salt and ground black pepper
300 ml/½ pint/1¼ cups single cream
300 ml/½ pint/1¼ cups milk

1 Lightly grease a large shallow ovenproof dish. Preheat the oven to 180°C/350°F/Gas 4.

2 Layer the potatoes with the onion and parsnips. In between each layer, dot the vegetables with garlic and butter, sprinkle over most of the cheese, add the nutmeg and season well.

3 Heat the cream and milk together in a saucepan until it is hot but not boiling. Slowly pour the creamy milk over the vegetables, making sure it seeps underneath them.

4 Scatter the remaining cheese over the vegetables and grate a little more nutmeg on top. Bake for about an hour or so until the potatoes are tender and the cheesey top is bubbling and golden.

Asparagus Mimosa

Pretty spears of fresh, tender asparagus are tossed in a buttery sauce and served with a chopped egg and chervil dressing. This also makes an excellent starter.

SERVES 2
225 g/8 oz fresh asparagus
salt
ground black pepper
50 g/2 oz/4 tbsp butter, melted
squeeze of fresh lemon juice
2 eggs, hard-boiled and chopped
15 ml/1 tbsp fresh chervil, chopped

1 Trim the asparagus stalks and peel off the tough outer layers at the base with a vegetable peeler.

2 Poach the asparagus spears in lightly salted water, until just tender. This will take between 3–6 minutes. (Use a clean, deep frying pan if you don't have an asparagus steamer.)

3 Drain the asparagus well and arrange it on two small plates or one large one. Season well.

4 Mix the melted butter with the lemon juice. Trickle over the spears, sprinkle with the eggs and garnish with the chervil. Serve warm.

Brussels Sprouts Stir-fry

Brussels sprouts are delicious when quickly stir-fried – they are really full-flavoured and their texture is full of crisp bite. Small Brussels sprouts have the best flavour.

SERVES 6

30 ml/2 tbsp groundnut or sunflower oil
450 g/1 lb small Brussels sprouts, trimmed
    and halved
3 spring onions, sliced
2 garlic cloves, crushed
1 small yellow pepper, sliced
30 ml/2 tbsp light soy sauce
15 ml/1 tbsp sesame seed oil
good pinch of granulated sugar
ground black pepper
30 ml/2 tbsp sesame seeds, toasted

1 Heat the oil in a wok until quite hot, then stir-fry the sprouts for 2 minutes.

2 Add the spring onions, garlic and yellow pepper and fry for another 2 minutes, stirring.

3 Toss in the soy sauce, sesame seed oil, sugar, and season with pepper. Scatter over the sesame seeds and serve hot immediately.

Hassleback Potatoes 🌿

These rather splendid roast potatoes are ideal to serve for dinner parties or special occasions such as Christmas. Use a good quality baking potato for the best results.

SERVES 4
olive or sunflower oil, for roasting
4 medium potatoes, peeled and halved
   lengthways
salt and ground black pepper
15 ml/1 tbsp natural colour dried
   breadcrumbs

1 Pour enough oil into a small roasting pan to just cover the base then put into an oven set at 200°C/400°F/Gas 6 to heat.

2 Meanwhile, par boil the potato halves for 5 minutes then drain. Cool slightly and slash about four times from the rounded tops almost down to the flat bottoms.

3 Place the potatoes in the heated roasting pan and spoon over the hot oil. Season well and return the potatoes to the oven for about 20 minutes.

4 Remove the potatoes once more from the oven, prise open the slashes slightly and spoon over the hot oil. Sprinkle the potato tops lightly with breadcrumbs and return to the oven for another 15 minutes or so until they are golden brown, cooked and crispy.

COOK'S TIP

There are many different ways of roasting potatoes in the oven. First, the choice of potato is important. Choose a variety which holds its shape well and yet is still slightly floury inside. Details on the pack or bag should give you guidance. The oil is important too – choose one which is either flavourless such as sunflower or groundnut oil or one with a lot of good flavour, such as olive oil. Just before serving, try trickling a little sesame seed, walnut or hazelnut oil over the roasted potatoes for a delicious nutty flavour.

Braised Fennel and Tomato

Fennel is a very undervalued vegetable but it is excellent cooked in a light tomato sauce. This dish can be gently simmered on the cooker or baked inside a moderate oven.

SERVES 4–6
2 fennel bulbs
1 small onion or 3 shallots, sliced
1 garlic clove, crushed
30 ml/2 tbsp olive oil
4 medium sized tomatoes, skinned and chopped
45 ml/3 tbsp dry white wine
15 ml/1 tbsp fresh marjoram, chopped
150 ml/¼ pint/⅔ cup stock or water
salt and ground black pepper

1 Trim the fennel then cut it into wedges. Reserve any fronds for a garnish.

2 Lightly sauté the fennel with the onion or shallots and garlic in the oil in a fireproof dish for 5 minutes.

3 Add the tomatoes, wine, marjoram and stock or water. Season.

4 Cover and either simmer very gently for 20 minutes, or bake in a preheated oven for 30 minutes at 190°C/375°F/Gas 5. Garnish with any reserved fronds and serve immediately.

Creamed Winter Vegetables

A mixture of chunky mashed root vegetables, such as carrots, parsnips and turnips or swedes, makes a wonderfully warming winter side dish.

SERVES 4–6
225 g/8 oz carrots, chopped
225 g/8 oz parsnips, chopped
1 small swede, chopped
25 g/1 oz/2 tbsp butter
10 ml/2 tsp mild curry paste
salt and ground black pepper
115 g/4 oz/½ cup fromage frais
15 ml/1 tbsp fresh chives, chopped

1 Boil the carrots, parsnips and swede in plenty of lightly salted water until tender. Drain the vegetables then return them to the pan with the butter, curry paste and seasoning.

2 Mash the vegetables lightly with a fork so that you end up with a chunky purée; you want to retain a good texture.

3 Stir in the fromage frais and chives. Check the seasoning and serve hot. This is a good dish to prepare in advance and reheat when required.

COOK'S TIP

Vegetable purées are a popular accompaniment with any dish which could be a little on the dry side, providing a good contrast of textures and colours. Suitable vegetables are Brussels sprouts, carrots, peas, broccoli and leeks.

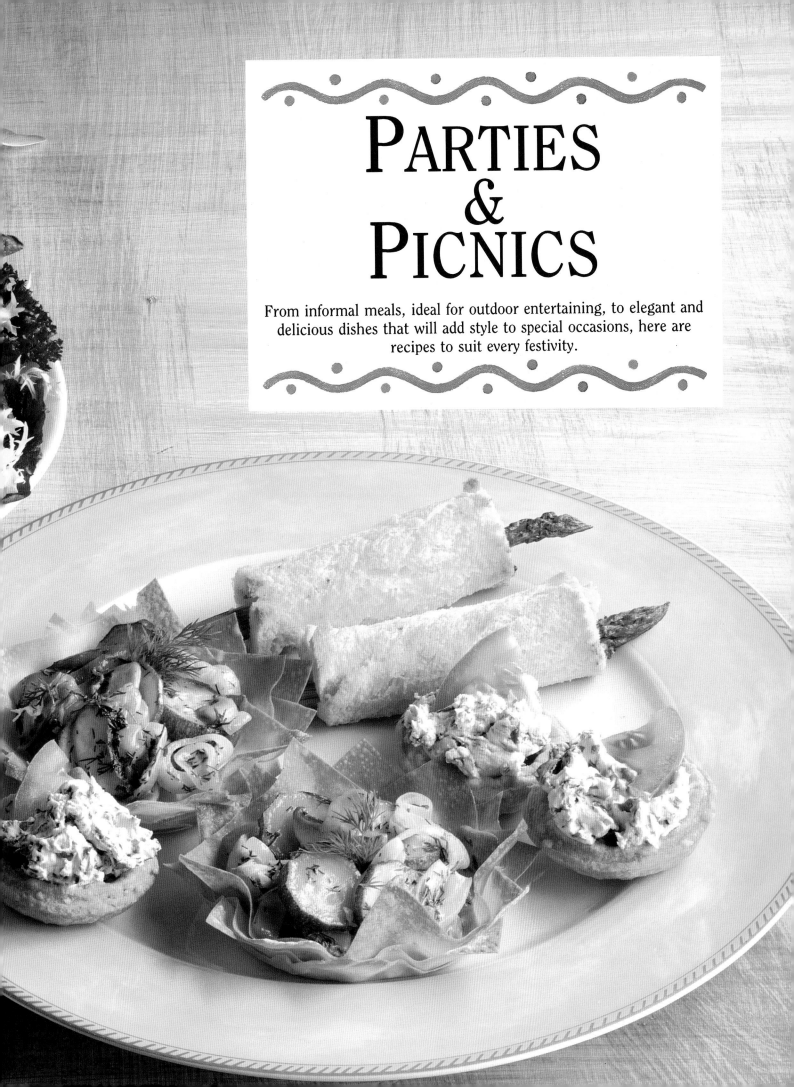

PARTIES
&
PICNICS

From informal meals, ideal for outdoor entertaining, to elegant and delicious dishes that will add style to special occasions, here are recipes to suit every festivity.

Spicy Potato Strudel

Wrap up a tasty mixture of vegetables in a spicy, creamy sauce with crisp filo pastry. It makes a perfect dish for a special family supper.

SERVES 4

1 onion, chopped
2 carrots, coarsely grated
1 courgette, chopped
350 g/12 oz potatoes, chopped
65 g/2½ oz/5 tbsp butter
10 ml/2 tsp mild curry paste
2.5 ml/½ tsp dried thyme
150 ml/¼ pint/⅔ cup water
salt and ground black pepper
1 egg, beaten
30 ml/2 tbsp single cream
50 g/2 oz Cheddar cheese, grated
8 sheets filo pastry
sesame seeds, to sprinkle

1 Fry the onion, carrots, courgette and potatoes in half the butter for 5 minutes until they are soft then add the curry paste and cook for a further minute.

2 Add the thyme, water and seasoning. Continue to cook gently, uncovered for another 10 minutes.

3 Allow the mixture to cool and mix in the egg, cream and cheese. Chill until ready to fill and roll.

4 Melt the remaining butter and lay out four sheets of filo pastry, slightly overlapping them to form a large rectangle. Brush with butter and fit the other sheets on top. Brush again.

5 Spoon the filling along one long edge, then roll up the pastry. Form it into a circle and brush again with the last of the butter. Sprinkle over the sesame seeds and set on a baking sheet.

6 Heat the oven to 190°C/375°F/Gas 5 then bake the strudel for about 25 minutes until golden and crisp. Allow to stand for 5 minutes or so before cutting.

Coronation Salad

This famous salad dressing was created especially for the coronation dinner of Queen Elizabeth II. It is a wonderful accompaniment to eggs and vegetables.

SERVES 6
450 g/1 lb new potatoes
salt
45 ml/3 tbsp vinaigrette dressing
3 spring onions, chopped
ground black pepper
6 eggs, hard-boiled and halved
frilly lettuce leaves, to serve
¼ cucumber, sliced then cut in shreds
6 large radishes, sliced
carton of salad cress
DRESSING
30 ml/2 tbsp olive oil
1 small onion, chopped
15 ml/1 tbsp mild curry
   powder or korma spice mix
10 ml/2 tsp tomato purée
30 ml/2 tbsp lemon juice
30 ml/2 tbsp sherry
300 ml/½ pint/1¼ cups mayonnaise
150 ml/¼ pint/¾ cup natural yogurt

1 Boil the potatoes in salted water until tender. Drain them and toss in the vinaigrette dressing.

2 Allow the potatoes to cool, stirring in the spring onions and seasoning. Cool the mixture thoroughly.

3 Meanwhile, make the coronation dressing. Heat the oil and fry the onion for 3 minutes until it is soft. Stir in the spice powder and fry for a further minute. Mix in all the other dressing ingredients.

4 Stir the dressing into the potatoes; add the eggs then chill. Line a serving platter with lettuce leaves and pile the salad in the centre. Scatter over the cucumber, radishes and cress.

Pasta and Wild Mushroom Mould

Bake pasta shapes in a golden crumb coating layered with a rich bechamel sauce and mushrooms. Scrumptious!

SERVES 4–6
200 g/7 oz pasta shapes
600 ml/1 pint/2½ cups milk
1 bay leaf
small onion stuck with 6 cloves
50 g/2 oz/4 tbsp butter
45 ml/3 tbsp breadcrumbs
10 ml/2 tsp dried mixed herbs
40 g/1½ oz/⅓ cup plain flour
60 ml/4 tbsp Parmesan cheese, freshly grated
fresh nutmeg, grated
salt and ground black pepper
2 eggs, beaten
1 × 15 g/½ oz pack porcini dried mushrooms
350 g/12 oz button mushrooms, sliced
2 garlic cloves, crushed
30 ml/2 tbsp olive oil
30 ml/ 2 tbsp fresh parsley, chopped

1 Boil the pasta according to the instructions on the pack. Drain and set aside. Heat the milk with the bay leaf and clove-studded onion and stand for 15 minutes. Remove bay leaf and onion.

2 Melt the butter in a saucepan and use a little to brush the inside of a large oval pie dish. Mix the crumbs and mixed herbs together and use them to coat the inside of the dish.

3 Stir the flour into the butter, cook for a minute then slowly add the hot milk to make a smooth sauce. Add the cheese, nutmeg, seasoning and cooked pasta. Cool for 5 minutes then beat in the eggs.

4 Soak the porcini in a little hot water until they are soft. Reserve the liquor and chop the porcini.

5 Fry the porcini with the sliced mushrooms and garlic in the olive oil for about 3 minutes. Season well, stir in the liquor and reduce down. Add the parsley.

6 Spoon a layer of pasta in the dish. Sprinkle over the mushrooms then more pasta and so on, finishing with pasta. Cover with greased foil. Heat the oven to 190°C/375°F/Gas 5 and bake for about 25–30 minutes. Allow to stand for 5 minutes before turning out to serve.

Aubergine Boats

These can be prepared ahead and baked prior to eating. The hazelnut topping contrasts nicely with the smooth aubergine filling.

SERVES 4
115 g/4 oz/⅔ cup brown basmati rice
2 medium size aubergines, halved lengthways
1 onion, chopped
2 garlic cloves, crushed
1 small green pepper, chopped
115 g/4 oz mushrooms, sliced
45 ml/3 tbsp olive oil
75 g/3 oz Cheddar cheese, grated
1 egg, beaten
2.5 ml/½ tsp marjoram
salt and ground black pepper
30 ml/2 tbsp hazelnuts, chopped

1 Boil the rice according to the instructions on the pack, drain and then cool. Scoop out the flesh from the aubergines and chop. Blanch the shells in boiling water for 2 minutes then drain upside down.

2 Fry the aubergine flesh, onion, garlic, pepper and mushrooms in the oil, for about 5 minutes.

3 Mix in the rice, cheese, egg, marjoram and seasoning. Arrange the aubergine shells in an ovenproof dish. Spoon the filling inside. Sprinkle over the nuts. Chill until ready to bake.

4 Heat the oven to 190°C/375°F/Gas 5 and bake the aubergines for about 25 minutes until the filling is set and the nuts are golden brown.

Chargrilled Vegetables with Salsa

Enjoy a barbecue with these chunky chargrilled vegetables. Serve hot with a no-cook salsa.

SERVES 4
1 large sweet potato, cut in thick slices
2 courgettes, halved lengthways
salt
2 red peppers, quartered
olive oil, to brush
SALSA
2 large tomatoes, skinned and finely chopped
2 spring onions, finely chopped
1 small green chilli, chopped
juice of 1 small lime
30 ml/2 tbsp fresh coriander, chopped
salt and ground black pepper

1 Par-boil the sweet potato for 5 minutes until it is barely tender. Drain and leave to cool.

2 Sprinkle the courgettes with a little salt and leave to drain in a colander for 20 minutes, then pat dry.

3 Make the salsa by mixing all the ingredients together, and allow them to stand for about 30 minutes to mellow.

4 Prepare the barbecue until the coals glow or preheat a grill. Brush the potato slices, courgettes and peppers with oil and cook them until they are lightly charred and softened, brushing with oil again and turning at least once. Serve hot accompanied by the salsa.

Garden Vegetable Terrine

Perfect for a special family picnic or buffet, this is a softly set, creamy terrine of colourful vegetables wrapped in glossy spinach leaves. Select large spinach leaves for the best results.

SERVES 6
225 g/8 oz fresh leaf spinach
3 carrots, cut in sticks
3–4 long, thin leeks
about 115 g/4 oz long green beans, topped and tailed
1 red pepper, cut in strips
2 courgettes, cut in sticks
115 g/4 oz broccoli florets
SAUCE
1 egg and 2 yolks
300 ml/½ pint/1¼ cups single cream
fresh nutmeg, grated
5 ml/1 tsp salt
50 g/2 oz Cheddar cheese, grated
oil, for greasing
ground black pepper

1 Blanch the spinach quickly in boiling water, then drain, refresh in cold water and drain again. Take care not to break up the leaves, then carefully pat them dry.

2 Grease a 1 kg/2 lb loaf tin and line the base with a sheet of greaseproof paper. Line the tin with the spinach leaves, trimming any thick stalks. Allow the leaves to overhang the tin.

3 Blanch the rest of the vegetables in boiling, salted water until just tender. Drain and refresh in cold water then, when cool, pat dry with pieces of kitchen paper towel.

4 Place the vegetables into the loaf tin in a colourful mixture, making sure the sticks of vegetables lie lengthways.

5 Beat the sauce ingredients together and slowly pour over the vegetables. Tap the loaf tin to ensure the sauce seeps into the gaps. Fold over the spinach leaves at the top of the terrine.

6 Cover the terrine with a sheet of greased foil then bake in a roasting pan half full of boiling water at 180°C/350°F/Gas 4 for about 1–1¼ hours until set.

7 Cool the terrine in the tin then chill. To serve, loosen the sides and shake gently out. Serve cut in thick slices.

Crêpe Galette

Make a stack of light pancakes and layer them together with a tasty lentil filling for an impressive dinner party main course. Serve with a homemade tomato sauce.

SERVES 6
115 g/4 oz/1 cup plain flour
good pinch of salt
1 egg
300 ml/½ pint/1¼ cups buttermilk, or milk and water, mixed
oil, for cooking
FILLING
2 leeks, thinly sliced
1 small fennel bulb, thinly sliced
60 ml/4 tbsp olive oil
150 g/6 oz/¾ cup red lentils
150 ml/¼ pint/⅔ cup dry white wine
1 × 400 g/14 oz can chopped tomatoes
300 ml/½ pint/1¼ cups stock
5 ml/1 tsp dried oregano
salt and ground black pepper
1 onion, sliced
225 g/8 oz mushrooms, sliced
225 g/8 oz frozen leaf spinach, thawed and squeezed dry
200 g/7 oz low fat cream cheese
50 g/2 oz Parmesan cheese, freshly grated

1 Make the pancake batter by mixing the flour, salt, egg and buttermilk or milk and water in a blender until smooth. Set aside while you prepare the filling.

2 Gently fry the leeks and fennel in half the olive oil for 5 minutes, then add the lentils and wine. Cook for a minute until reduced down then stir in the tomatoes and stock.

3 Bring the leek/fennel mixture to a boil, add the oregano and seasoning then simmer for 20 minutes, stirring it occasionally until it thickens.

4 Fry the onion and mushrooms in the remaining olive oil for 5 minutes, stir in the spinach and heat. Season well then mix in the cream cheese.

5 Make about 12–14 pancakes with the batter in a well heated non-stick frying pan. Lightly grease a 20 cm/8 in round deep spring-form cake tin and line the base and sides with some of the pancakes, overlapping them as necessary.

6 Layer the remaining pancakes with the two fillings, sprinkling Parmesan in between and pressing them down well. Finish with a pancake on top.

7 Cover with foil and set aside to rest. Preheat the oven to 190°C/375°F/Gas 5. Bake for about 40 minutes, then turn out and allow to firm up for 10 minutes before cutting into wedges.

COOK'S TIP

This can be frozen ready made up, but it is probably nicer if frozen in parts – the pancakes interleaved with greaseproof paper and then wrapped in foil and the sauce frozen separately.

Polenta Fingers with Beans and Tomatoes

Polenta, or cornmeal, is a popular family favourite in Italy. It is eaten either hot from a bowl or allowed to set, cut into fingers, and grilled.

SERVES 6
1.75 litres/3 pints/7½ cups milk and
    water, mixed
10 ml/2 tsp salt
275 g/10 oz/1½ cups polenta
25 g/1 oz/2 tbsp butter, plus extra for
    spreading
50 g/2 oz Parmesan cheese, freshly grated
ground black pepper
SAUCE
1 onion, chopped
2 garlic cloves, crushed
30 ml/2 tbsp olive oil
1 × 400 g/14 oz can chopped tomatoes
salt and ground black pepper
good pinch of dried sage
225 g/8 oz frozen broad beans

1 In a large saucepan, bring the milk and water to a boil. Stir in the salt. While stirring with a wooden spoon trickle the polenta into the boiling liquid in a steady stream and continue stirring until the mixture has thickened.

2 Lower the heat and simmer for about 20 minutes, stirring frequently. Add the butter, cheese and seasoning.

3 Lightly grease a shallow roasting pan and pour in the polenta mixture. Cool, then chill overnight.

4 For the sauce, fry the onion and garlic in the oil for 5 minutes. Add the tomatoes, seasoning and sage and cook for a further 10 minutes. Stir in the broad beans and cook for 5 minutes more.

5 Turn out the polenta and cut into fingers. Grill both sides until brown and crisp. Spread with a little butter and serve accompanied by the tomato and beans.

Paprika and Parmesan Tartlets

Pretty pink pastry tarts with a tangy cream filling are ideal for handing round at drinks parties. Make the cases ahead of the party and fill them just before serving.

MAKES 18
225 g/8 oz/2 cups plain flour
10 ml/2 tsp paprika
150 g/5 oz/10 tbsp butter or sunflower
    margarine
40 g/1½ oz Parmesan cheese, freshly
    grated
cold water, to bind
FILLING
350 g/12 oz goats' cheese
50 g/2 oz rocket leaves, or watercress,
    chopped
30 ml/2 tbsp fresh chives, chopped
salt and ground black pepper
450 g/1 lb tomatoes, sliced

1 Sift the flour with the paprika and rub in the butter or margarine. Stir in the Parmesan and mix to a firm dough with cold water.

2 Roll out the pastry and stamp out 18 rounds, large enough to fit into bun tins. Prick the bases well with a fork and chill while you preheat the oven to 190°C/375°F/Gas 5.

3 Bake the tartlets for 15 minutes until crisp. Cool them on a wire rack.

4 Beat the cheese with the rocket or cress, chives and seasoning. Slice the tomatoes, allowing roughly two slices per tart.

5 When ready to serve, spoon the filling into the tarts. Top each one with some tomato and garnish with extra rocket or cress leaves.

Tofu Satay

Grill cubes of tofu until crispy then serve with a Thai-style peanut sauce. Soaking the sticks helps them withstand the hot grilling.

SERVES 4—6
2 × 200 g/7 oz packs smoked tofu
45 ml/3 tbsp light soy sauce
10 ml/2 tsp sesame oil
1 garlic clove, crushed
1 yellow and 1 red pepper, cut in squares
8—12 fresh bay leaves
sunflower oil, for grilling
SAUCE
2 spring onions, finely chopped
2 garlic cloves, crushed
good pinch chilli powder or few drops hot chilli sauce
5 ml/1 tsp granulated sugar
15 ml/1 tbsp white vinegar
30 ml/2 tbsp light soy sauce
45 ml/3 tbsp crunchy peanut butter

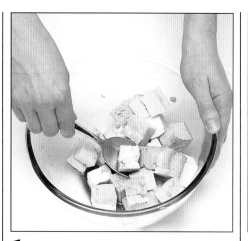

1 Soak 8—12 wooden satay sticks in water for 20 minutes then drain. Cut the tofu into bite-sized cubes and mix with the soy sauce, sesame oil and garlic. Cover and marinate for 20 minutes.

2 Beat the sauce ingredients together until well blended. Avoid using a food processor for this as the texture should be slightly chunky.

3 Drain the tofu and thread the cubes onto the soaked sticks with the pepper squares and bay leaves. Larger leaves may need to be halved.

4 Heat a grill or barbecue until quite hot. Brush the satays with oil. Grill, turning the sticks occasionally, until the ingredients are browned and crisp. Serve hot with the dipping sauce.

Party Mousaka

Always a popular favourite for both guests and the cook at parties, mousaka is ideal because it benefits from being made ahead of time, requiring just reheating on the day.

SERVES 8

2 large aubergines, thinly sliced
6 courgettes, cut in chunks
150 ml/¼ pint/⅔ cup olive oil, plus extra if required
675 g/1½ lb potatoes, thinly sliced
2 onions, sliced
3 garlic cloves, crushed
150 ml/¼ pint/⅔ cup dry white wine
2 × 400 g/14 oz cans chopped tomatoes
30 ml/2 tbsp tomato purée
1 × 430 g/15 oz can green lentils
10 ml/2 tsp dried oregano
60 ml/4 tbsp fresh parsley, chopped
225 g/8 oz/2 cups feta cheese, crumbled
salt and ground black pepper

BECHAMEL SAUCE

40 g/1½ oz/3 tbsp butter
40 g/1½ oz/4 tbsp plain flour
600 ml/1 pint/2½ cups milk
2 eggs, beaten
115 g/4 oz Parmesan cheese, grated
nutmeg, freshly grated

1 Lightly salt the aubergines and courgettes in a colander and leave them to drain for 30 minutes. Rinse and pat dry.

2 Heat the oil until quite hot in a frying pan and quickly brown the aubergine and courgette slices. Remove them with a slotted spoon and drain on a kitchen paper towel. This step is important to cut down on the oiliness of the aubergine. Next, brown the potato slices, remove and pat dry. Add the onion and garlic to the pan with a little extra oil, if required, and fry until lightly browned – 3–5 minutes.

3 Pour in the wine and cook until reduced down then add the tomatoes and lentils plus the liquor from the can. Stir in the herbs and season well. Cover and simmer for 15 minutes.

4 In a large ovenproof dish, layer the vegetables, trickling the tomato and lentil sauce in between and scattering over the feta cheese. Finish with a layer of aubergine slices.

5 Cover the vegetables with a sheet of foil and bake at 190°C/375°F/Gas 5 for 25 minutes or until the vegetables are quite soft but not overcooked.

6 Meanwhile, for the bechamel sauce, put the butter, flour and milk into a saucepan all together and bring slowly to a boil, stirring or whisking constantly. It should thicken and become smooth. Season and add the nutmeg.

7 Remove the sauce and cool for 5 minutes then beat in the eggs. Pour over the aubergines and sprinkle with the Parmesan. If cooking ahead, cool and chill at this stage.

8 To finish, return to the oven uncovered and bake for a further 25–30 minutes until golden and bubbling hot.

Basmati and Blue Lentil Salad

Puy lentils from France (sometimes known as blue lentils) are small, deliciously nutty pulses, highly prized by gourmets. They blend beautifully with aromatic basmati rice.

SERVES 6
115 g/4 oz/⅔ cup puys de dome lentils, soaked
225 g/8 oz/1¼ cups basmati rice, rinsed well
2 carrots, coarsely grated
⅓ cucumber, halved, seeded and coarsely grated
3 spring onions, sliced
45 ml/3 tbsp fresh parsley, chopped
DRESSING
30 ml/2 tbsp sunflower oil
30 ml/2 tbsp extra virgin olive oil
30 ml/2 tbsp wine vinegar
30 ml/2 tbsp fresh lemon juice
good pinch of granulated sugar
salt and ground black pepper

1 Soak the lentils for 30 minutes. Meanwhile, make the dressing by shaking all the ingredients together in a screw-topped jar. Set aside.

2 Boil the lentils in plenty of unsalted water for 20–25 minutes or until soft. Drain thoroughly.

3 Boil the basmati rice for 10 minutes, then drain.

4 Mix together the rice and lentils in the dressing and season well. Leave to cool.

5 Add the carrots, cucumber, onions and parsley. Spoon into an attractive serving bowl and chill before serving.

Wild Rice with Julienne Vegetables

Make an accompanying dish more interesting with some exquisite wild rice. For the best flavour, buy a good quality wild rice (which is actually a cereal!) and, to shorten the cooking time, soak it overnight.

SERVES 4
115 g/4 oz/½ cup wild rice
1 red onion, sliced
2 carrots, cut in julienne sticks
2 celery sticks, cut in julienne sticks
50 g/2 oz/4 tbsp butter
150 ml/¼ pint/⅔ cup stock or water
salt and ground black pepper
2 medium courgettes, cut in thicker sticks
a few toasted almond flakes, to serve

1 Drain the soaked rice, then boil in plenty of unsalted water for 15–20 minutes, until it is soft and many of the grains have burst open. Drain.

2 In another saucepan, gently fry the onion, carrots and celery in the butter for 2 minutes then pour in the stock or water and season well.

3 Bring to a boil, simmer for 2 minutes then stir in the courgettes. Cook for 1 more minute then mix in the rice. Reheat and serve hot sprinkled with the almonds.

Oven-Crisp Asparagus Rolls

A lovely treat when fresh asparagus is in season is to wrap blanched spears in slices of thin bread and bake in a buttery glaze until crisp. Out of season, use canned or frozen spears.

SERVES 8
8 thick spears of fresh asparagus
salt
115 g/4 oz/8½ tbsp butter, softened
15 ml/1 tbsp coarse grained mustard
grated rind of 1 lemon
ground black pepper
8 slices thin white bread, crusts removed

1 Trim the asparagus stalks, peeling the tough woody skin at the base. Blanch until just tender in a shallow pan of boiling, salted water. Drain and refresh in cold water. Pat dry.

2 Blend two-thirds of the butter with the mustard, lemon rind and seasoning. Spread over the slices of bread.

3 Lay an asparagus spear on the edge of each bread slice and roll it up tightly. Place the rolls join side down on a lightly greased baking sheet.

4 Melt the remaining butter and brush over the rolls. Heat the oven to 190°C/375°F/Gas 5 and bake for 12–15 minutes until golden and crisp. Cool slightly before serving.

VARIATION

Asparagus has always been something of a luxury as its season is so short, but imports from across the world mean that it is available almost all year round, albeit at a price!

Thin baby asparagus, known as sprue, can be eaten raw in salads or stir-fried quickly. Opinions differ about the merits of green or white asparagus spears. The latter are forced in the dark (hence their white colour), but some people consider them to have a better flavour and texture.

Ratatouille Tart

Serve this pretty tart warm so the cheese is easy to cut and eat. For the best results, make the base and filling separately then heat and combine just before serving.

SERVES 6
115 g/4 oz/1 cup plain flour
115 g/4 oz/¾ cup wholemeal flour
5 ml/1 tsp dried mixed herbs
salt and ground black pepper
115 g/4 oz/½ cup sunflower margarine
45–60 ml/3–4 tbsp cold water
FILLING
1 small aubergine, thickly sliced
salt
45 ml/3 tbsp olive oil
1 onion, sliced
1 red or yellow pepper, sliced
2 garlic cloves, crushed
2 courgettes, thickly sliced
2 tomatoes, skinned and sliced
ground black pepper
30 ml/2 tbsp fresh basil, chopped
150 g/5 oz Mozzarella cheese, sliced
30 ml/2 tbsp pine nuts

1 Mix the two flours with the herbs and seasoning then rub in the margarine until it resembles fine crumbs. Mix to a firm dough with water.

2 Roll out the pastry and line a 23 cm/ 9 in round flan tin. Prick the base, line with foil and baking beans then allow to rest in the fridge.

3 Meanwhile, sprinkle the aubergine lightly with salt and leave to drain for 30 minutes in a colander. Rinse and pat dry.

4 Heat the oil in a frying pan and fry the onion and pepper for 5 minutes, then add the garlic, courgettes and aubergine. Fry for a further 10 minutes, stirring the mixture occasionally.

5 Stir in the tomatoes and seasoning, cook for a further 3 minutes, add the basil then remove the pan from the heat and allow to cool.

6 Heat the oven to 200°C/400°F/Gas 6. Place the flan on a baking sheet and bake for 25 minutes, removing the foil and baking beans for the last 5 minutes. Cool and then, if possible, remove the case from the tin.

7 When ready to serve, spoon the vegetables into the case using a slotted spoon so any juices drain off and don't soak into the pastry. Top with the cheese slices and pine nuts. Toast under a preheated grill until golden and bubbling. Serve warm.

Filo Baskets with Ginger Dill Vegetables

Make up some elegant filo baskets, then fill with some crisply steamed vegetables tossed in an interesting and tasty sauce.

SERVES 4
4 sheets of filo pastry
40 g/1½ oz/3 tbsp butter, melted
FILLING
30 ml/2 tbsp olive oil
15 ml/1 tbsp fresh root ginger, grated
2 garlic cloves, crushed
3 shallots, sliced
225 g/8 oz mushrooms, chestnut or brown, sliced
115 g/4 oz oyster mushrooms, sliced
1 courgette, sliced
200 g/7 oz crème fraîche
30 ml/2 tbsp fresh dill, chopped
salt and ground black pepper
dill and parsley sprigs, to serve

1 Cut the filo sheets into four. Line four Yorkshire pudding tins, angling the layers so that the corners form a pretty star shape. Brush between each layer with butter. Set aside.

2 Heat the oven to 190°C/375°F/Gas 5. Bake the cases for about 10 minutes until golden brown and crisp. Remove and cool.

3 For the filling, heat the oil and sauté the ginger, garlic and shallots for 2 minutes, then add the mushrooms and courgette. Cook for another 3 minutes.

4 Mix in the crème fraîche, chopped dill and seasoning. Heat until just bubbling then spoon into the filo cases. Garnish with the dill and parsley and serve.

Gado Gado Salad with Peanut Sambal

Indonesians enjoy a salad of lightly-steamed vegetables topped with a peanut sauce. It is ideal for a colourful summer buffet dish.

SERVES 6
225 g/8 oz new potatoes, halved
2 carrots, cut in sticks
115 g/4 oz green beans
½ small cauliflower, broken into florets
¼ firm white cabbage, shredded
200 g/7 oz bean or lentil sprouts
4 eggs, hard-boiled and quartered
bunch watercress, trimmed
SAUCE
90 ml/6 tbsp crunchy peanut butter
300 ml/½ pint/1¼ cups cold water
1 garlic clove, crushed
30 ml/2 tbsp dark soy sauce
15 ml/1 tbsp dry sherry
10 ml/2 tsp caster sugar
15 ml/1 tbsp fresh lemon juice
5 ml/1 tsp anchovy essence

1 Fit a steamer or metal colander over a pan of gently boiling water. Cook the potatoes for 10 minutes.

2 Add the rest of the vegetables and sprouts and steam for a further 10 minutes until tender. Cool and serve on a platter with the egg quarters surrounded by the watercress.

3 Beat all the sauce ingredients together until smooth. Put the sauce in a small bowl and drizzle over each individual serving of salad.

Persian Rice and Lentils with a Tahdeeg

Persian or Iran cuisine is an exotic and delicious one, steeped in history. Flavours are intense and exotic, and somehow more sophisticated than other Mediterranean styles. A tahdeeg is the glorious, golden rice crust that forms at the bottom of the saucepan.

SERVES 8
450 g/1 lb basmati rice, rinsed thoroughly
   and soaked
2 onions, 1 chopped, 1 thinly sliced
2 garlic cloves, crushed
150 ml/¼ pint/⅔ cup sunflower oil
150 g/5 oz/1 cup green lentils, soaked
600 ml/1 pint/2½ cups stock
50 g/2 oz/⅓ cup raisins
10 ml/2 tsp ground coriander
45 ml/3 tbsp tomato purée
salt and ground black pepper
few strands of saffron
1 egg yolk, beaten
10 ml/2 tsp natural yogurt
75 g/3 oz/6 tbsp butter, melted and
   strained
extra oil, for frying

1 Boil the rinsed and drained rice in plenty of well salted water for 3 minutes only. Drain again.

2 Meanwhile, fry the chopped onion and garlic in 30 ml/2 tbsp of oil for 5 minutes then add the lentils, stock, raisins, coriander, tomato purée and seasoning. Bring to a boil, then cover and simmer for 20 minutes. Set aside.

3 Soak the saffron strands in a little hot water. Remove about 120 ml/8 tbsp of the rice and mix with the egg yolk and yogurt. Season well.

4 In a large saucepan, heat about two-thirds of the remaining oil and scatter the egg and yogurt rice evenly over the base.

5 Scatter the remaining rice into the pan, alternating it with the lentils. Build up in a pyramid shape away from the sides of the pan, finishing with plain rice on top.

6 With a long wooden spoon handle, make three holes down to the bottom of the pan and drizzle over the butter. Bring to a high heat, then wrap the pan lid in a clean, wet tea towel and place firmly on top. When a good head of steam appears, turn the heat down to low. Cook for about 30 minutes.

7 Meanwhile, fry the sliced onion in the remaining oil until browned and crisp. Drain well and set aside.

8 Remove the rice pan from the heat, still covered and stand it briefly in a sink of cold water for a minute or two to loosen the base. Remove the lid and mix a few spoons of the white rice with the saffron water prepared in Step 3.

9 Toss the rice and lentils together in the pan and spoon out onto a serving dish in a mound. Scatter the saffron rice on top. Break up the rice crust on the bottom (the prized tahdeeg) and place around the mound. Scatter the onions on top of the saffron rice and serve.

Vegetable Fritters with Tzatziki

Spicy deep-fried aubergine and courgette slices served with a creamy Greek yogurt and dill dip make a good, simple party starter or an excellent side dish.

SERVES 4–6
½ cucumber, coarsely grated
225 g/8 oz Greek natural yogurt
15 ml/1 tbsp extra virgin olive oil
10 ml/2 tsp fresh lemon juice
30 ml/2 tbsp fresh dill, chopped
15 ml/1 tbsp fresh mint, chopped
1 garlic clove, crushed
salt and ground black pepper
1 large aubergine, thickly sliced
2 courgettes, thickly sliced
1 egg white, beaten
40 g/1½ oz/4 tbsp plain flour
10 ml/2 tsp ground coriander
ground cumin

1 For the dip, mix the cucumber, yogurt, oil, lemon juice, dill, mint, garlic and seasoning. Spoon into a bowl then set aside.

2 Layer the aubergine and courgettes in a colander and sprinkle them with salt. Leave for 30 minutes. Rinse in cold water then pat dry.

3 Put the egg white into a bowl. Mix the flour, coriander and cumin with seasoning and put into another bowl.

4 Dip the vegetables first into the egg white then into the seasoned flour and set aside.

5 Heat about 2.5 cm/1 in of oil in a deep frying pan until quite hot, then fry the vegetables a few at a time until they are golden and crisp.

6 Drain and keep warm while you fry the remainder. Serve warm on a platter with a bowl of the tzatziki dip lightly sprinkled with paprika.

Mushroom Saucers

Recipes which are already portioned are a great boon for the host, as guests can help themselves without feeling they are taking more than their fair share. Large flat mushrooms are great for this reason.

SERVES 8
8 large flat mushrooms with stalks removed, wiped clean and chopped
45 ml/3 tbsp olive oil
salt and ground black pepper
1 onion, sliced
5 ml/1 tsp cumin seeds
450 g/1 lb leaf spinach, stalks trimmed, and shredded
1 × 425 g/15 oz can red kidney beans, drained
1 × 200 g/7 oz pack soft cheese with garlic and herbs
2 medium tomatoes, halved, seeded and sliced in strips

1 Heat the oven to 190°C/375°F/Gas 5. Lightly grease a large, shallow ovenproof dish. Brush the mushrooms with some oil, place them in the dish and season well. Cover with foil and bake for 15–20 minutes. Uncover, drain and reserve the juices.

2 Fry the onion and chopped mushroom stalks in the remaining oil for 5 minutes until soft. Then add the cumin seeds and mushroom juices and cook for a minute longer until reduced down.

3 Stir in the spinach and fry until the leaves begin to wilt, then mix in the beans and heat well. Add the cheese, stirring until melted and season again.

4 Divide the mixture between the mushroom cups and return to the oven to heat through. Serve garnished with tomato slices.

Birds' Nests

A recipe from an old hand-written cookery book dated 1887. These are also known as Welsh Eggs because they resemble Scotch Eggs but they have leeks in the filling. They are ideal for taking on picnics.

SERVES 6
6 eggs, hard-boiled
flour, seasoned with salt and paprika
1 leek, chopped
10 ml/2 tsp sunflower oil
115 g/4 oz/2 cups fresh white
  breadcrumbs
grated rind and juice of 1 lmeon
50 g/2 oz/½ cup vegetarian shredded suet
60 ml/4 tbsp fresh parsley, chopped
5 ml/1 tsp dried thyme
salt and ground black pepper
1 egg, beaten
75 g/3 oz/½ cup dried breadcrumbs
oil, for deep fat frying
lettuce and tomato slices, to garnish

1 Peel the hard-boiled eggs and toss in the seasoned flour.

2 Fry the leeks in the oil for about 3 minutes. Remove, cool, then mix with the fresh breadcrumbs, lemon rind and juice, suet, herbs and seasoning. If the mixture is a little dry add a little water.

3 Shape the mixture around the eggs, then toss first into the beaten egg, then the dried breadcrumbs. Set aside on a plate to chill for 30 minutes.

4 Pour enough oil to fill one-third of a deep fat fryer and heat to a temperature of 190°C/375°F, and fry the eggs, three at a time, for about 3 minutes. Remove and drain on kitchen paper towel.

5 Serve, cool, cut in half on a platter lined with lettuce and garnished with tomato slices.

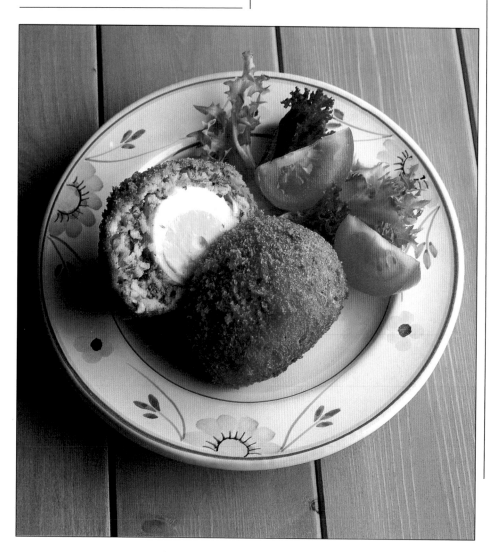

Portable Salads

A clever Victorian notion for transporting saucy salads neatly to a picnic site was to pack them in a hollowed out loaf of bread.

SERVES 6
1 large, deep crusty loaf
softened butter or margarine, for spreading
few leaves of crisp lettuce
4 eggs, hardboiled and chopped
350g/12 oz new potatoes, boiled and sliced
1 green pepper, thinly sliced
2 carrots, coarsely grated
3 spring onions, chopped
115 g/4 oz Gouda cheese, grated
salt and ground black pepper
DRESSING
30 ml/2 tbsp mayonnaise
30 ml/2 tbsp natural yogurt
30 ml/2 tbsp milk
1 garlic clove, crushed (optional)
15 ml/1 tbsp fresh dill, chopped

1 Cut the top from the loaf and scoop out the bread inside. Use this for making fresh breadcrumbs and freeze for later.

2 Spread the inside of the loaf lightly with the softened butter or margarine, then line with the lettuce leaves.

3 Mix the eggs with the vegetables and cheese. Season well. Beat the dressing ingredients together and mix into the egg and vegetables.

4 Spoon the dressed salad into the hollow and lined loaf, replace the lid and wrap in cling film. Chill until ready to transport. To serve, spoon the salad onto plates and cut the crust into chunks.

Marbled Quails' Eggs

Hard-boiled quails' eggs re-boiled in smoky China tea assume a pretty marbled skin. It's quite a treat to dip them into a fragrant spicy salt and hand them round with drinks. Szechuan peppercorns can be bought from Oriental food stores.

SERVES 4–6
12 quails' eggs
600 ml/1 pint/2½ cups strong lapsang souchong tea
15 ml/1 tbsp dark soy sauce
15 ml/1 tbsp dry sherry
2 star anise pods
lettuce leaves, to serve
milled Szechuan red peppercorns
sea salt, to mix

1 Place the quails' eggs in cold water and bring to the boil. Time them for 2 minutes from when the water boils.

2 Remove the eggs from the pan and run them under cold water to cool. Tap the shells all over so they are crazed, but do not peel yet.

3 In a saucepan, bring the tea to the boil and add the soy sauce, sherry and star anise. Re-boil the eggs for about 15 minutes, partially covered, so the liquid does not boil dry.

4 Cool the eggs, then peel them and arrange on a small platter lined with lettuce leaves. Mix the ground red peppercorns with equal quantities of salt and place in a small side dish.

Beetroot Roulade

This roulade is simple to make, yet will create a stunning impression. Prepare it in the autumn when beetroots are at their best.

SERVES 6
225 g/8 oz fresh beetroot, cooked and peeled
2.5 ml/½ tsp ground cumin
25 g/1 oz/2 tbsp butter
10 ml/2 tsp grated onion
4 eggs, separated
salt and ground black pepper
FILLING
150 ml/¼ pint/⅔ cup crème frâiche or double cream
10 ml/2 tsp white wine vinegar
good pinch dry mustard powder
5 ml/1 tsp sugar
45 ml/3 tbsp fresh parsley, chopped
30 ml/2 tbsp fresh dill, chopped
45 ml/3 tbsp horseradish relish

1 Line and grease a Swiss roll tin. Preheat the oven to 190°C/375°F/Gas 5.

2 Roughly chop the beetroot then blend to a purée in a food processor and beat in the cumin, butter, onion, egg yolks and seasoning. Turn the beetroot purée into a large bowl.

3 In another bowl, that is spotlessly clean, whisk the egg whites until they form soft peaks. Fold them into the beetroot mixture carefully.

4 Spoon the mixture into the Swiss roll tin, level and bake for about 15 minutes until just firm to touch.

5 Have ready a clean tea towel laid over a wire rack. Turn the beetroot out onto the towel, and remove the paper carefully in strips.

6 Beat the crème frâiche or cream until lightly stiff, then fold in the remaining ingredients. Spread this mixture onto the beetroot. Roll up the roulade in the towel and allow it to cool.

Pan Bagna

You need three essential elements for this French picnic classic: a really fresh French baguette, ripe juicy tomatoes, full of flavour and good, extra virgin olive oil. It is ideal to pack for a picnic.

SERVES 3–4
1 long French stick, split in half
1 garlic clove, halved
60–90 ml/4–6 tbsp extra virgin olive oil
3–4 ripe tomatoes, thinly sliced
salt and ground black pepper
1 small green pepper, thinly sliced
50 g/2 oz Gruyère cheese, thinly sliced
a few stoned black olives, sliced
6 fresh basil leaves

1 Rub the cut surface of the bread with the garlic and discard the clove. Brush over half of the olive oil on both halves of the bread.

2 Lay the tomato slices on top, season well and top with the pepper. Drizzle over the remaining oil.

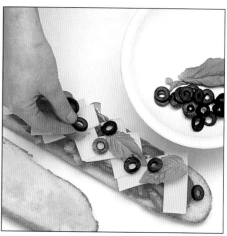

3 Top the tomatoes with the cheese slices, olives and basil leaves. Sandwich the loaf together firmly and wrap it in cling film for an hour or more. Serve cut diagonally in thick slices.

Sandwiches, Rolls and Fillings

There is an increasing variety of wonderful breads and rolls now for the picnic packer to choose from – not only variations on white and wholemeal breads, but also flavoured breads such as onion, walnut, tomato swirl and black olive. Make sure the breads are fresh and spread them right up to the edges using good butter or a quality margarine spread. Once filled, wrap in cling film and chill until required. However, many a good sandwich is spoiled if served too cold, so allow it to return to room temperature before eating.

FILLING IDEAS
Unless specified, keep the fillings in separate layers rather than mixing the ingredients together.

☐ De-rinded Brie or Camembert, mixed with chopped walnuts or pecans and served with *frisée* or curly endive lettuce.

☐ Yeast extract, scrambled egg (made without milk) and bean sprout (especially good with alfalfa sprouts). Spread the bread or roll with yeast extract rather than mixing it into the egg.

☐ Fry onions in olive oil until crisp and brown. Cool. Layer with shredded, young raw spinach leaves and grated cheese mixed with a little mayonnaise.

☐ **Real English Cucumber Sandwiches.** Peel strips from a whole cucumber to leave it stripy, then slice thinly on a mandoline or a food processor slicer. Sprinkle lightly with salt and leave to drain for 30 minutes in a colander. Pat dry. Sprinkle lightly with a little vinegar and black pepper. Sandwich in very fresh white or wheatmeal bread and cut off the crusts. Cut into small triangles.

Pasta and Beetroot Salad

Colour is vital at a party table, and this salad is certainly eye catching. Serve the egg and avocado at the last moment to avoid discoloration.

SERVES 8
2 uncooked beetroots, scrubbed
225 g/8 oz pasta shells or twists
45 ml/3 tbsp vinaigrette dressing
salt and ground black pepper
2 celery sticks, thinly sliced
3 spring onions, sliced
75 g/3 oz/⅔ cup walnuts or hazelnuts, roughly chopped
1 dessert apple, cored, halved and sliced
DRESSING
60 ml/4 tbsp mayonnaise
45 ml/3 tbsp natural yogurt or fromage frais
30 ml/2 tbsp milk
10 ml/2 tsp horseradish relish
TO SERVE
curly lettuce leaves
3 eggs, hard boiled and chopped
2 ripe avocadoes
box of salad cress

1 Boil the beetroots, without peeling them, in lightly salted water until they are just tender. Drain, cool, peel and chop. Set aside.

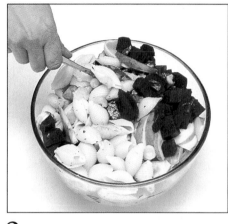

2 Cook the pasta according to the instructions on the pack then drain and toss in the vinaigrette and season well. Cool. Mix the pasta with the beetroot, celery, onions, nuts and apple.

3 Stir all the dressing ingredients together and mix into the pasta bowl. Chill well.

4 To serve, line a pretty salad bowl with the lettuce leaves and pile the salad in the centre. When ready to serve, scatter over the chopped egg. Peel and slice the avocadoes and arrange them on top then sprinkle over the cress.

Gazpacho

This classic Spanish no-cook soup is ideal for taking on picnics as it can be packed straight from the refrigerator. Keep the chopped vegetables in separate pots and hand them round as an accompaniment.

SERVES 6
1 slice white bread, crusts removed
cold water, to soak
1 garlic clove, crushed
30 ml/2 tbsp extra virgin olive oil
30 ml/2 tbsp white wine vinegar
6 large ripe tomatoes, skinned and finely chopped
1 small onion, finely chopped
2.5 ml/½ tsp paprika
good pinch ground cumin
150 ml/¼ pint/⅔ cup tomato juice
salt and ground black pepper
TO GARNISH
1 green pepper, chopped
⅓ cucumber, peeled, seeded and chopped
CROÛTONS
2 slices bread, cubed and deep fried

1 Soak the bread slice in enough cold water just to cover and leave for about 5 minutes, then mash with a fork.

2 Pound the garlic, oil and vinegar with a pestle and mortar or blend in a food processor. Mix this into the bread.

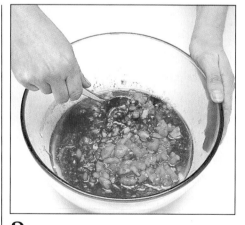

3 Spoon the mixture into a bowl and stir in the tomatoes, onion, spices and tomato juice. Season well and store in the refrigerator. Prepare the garnishes and store these in separate containers.

4 For a picnic, pour the chilled soup into a flask. Otherwise, pour into a chilled glass salad bowl and hand the garnishes round in smaller bowls.

Sesame Egg Roll

A Japanese-inspired idea. An egg pancake is rolled up with a creamy watercress filling and served cut in thick slices.

SERVES 3–4
3 eggs
15 ml/1 tbsp soy sauce
15 ml/1 tbsp sesame seeds
5 ml/1 tsp sesame seed oil
salt and ground black pepper
15 ml/1 tbsp sunflower oil
75 g/3 oz cream cheese with garlic
1 bunch watercress, chopped

1 Beat the eggs with the soy sauce, sesame seeds, sesame seed oil and seasoning.

2 Heat the sunflower oil in a large frying pan until quite hot, then pour in the egg mixture, tilting the pan so it covers the whole base. Cook until firm.

3 Allow the pancake to stand in the pan for a few minutes then turn out onto a chopping board and cool completely.

4 Beat the cream cheese until soft, season well then mix in the chopped watercress. Spread this over the egg pancake then roll it up quite firmly. Wrap in cling film and chill.

Homemade Coleslaw

Forget shop-bought coleslaw! Making your own at home is quite quick and easy to do – and it tastes fresh, crunchy and wonderful.

SERVES 4–6
¼ firm white cabbage
1 small onion, finely chopped
2 celery sticks, thinly sliced
2 carrots, coarsely grated
5–10 ml/1–2 tsp caraway seeds (optional)
1 dessert apple, cored and chopped (optional)
50 g/2 oz/½ cup walnuts, chopped (optional)
salt and ground black pepper
DRESSING
45 ml/3 tbsp mayonnaise
30 ml/2 tbsp single cream or natural yogurt
5 ml/1 tsp lemon rind, grated
salt and ground black pepper

1 Cut and discard the core from the cabbage quarter then shred the leaves finely. Place this in a large bowl.

2 Into the cabbage, toss the onion, celery and carrot, plus the caraway seeds, apple and walnuts, if using. Season well.

3 Mix the dressing ingredients together and stir into the vegetables. Cover and allow to stand for 2 hours, stirring occasionally, then chill the coleslaw lightly before serving.

Malfatti with Red Sauce

If you ever felt dumplings were a little heavy, try making these light Italian spinach and ricotta malfatti instead. Serve them with a simple tomato and red pepper sauce.

SERVES 4–6
450 g/1 lb fresh leaf spinach, stalks trimmed
1 small onion, chopped
1 garlic clove, crushed
15 ml/1 tbsp olive oil
400 g/14 oz ricotta cheese
75 g/3 oz/⅔ cup dried breadcrumbs
50 g/2 oz/½ cup plain flour
5 ml/1 tsp salt
50 g/2 oz Parmesan cheese, freshly grated
fresh nutmeg, grated, to taste
3 eggs, beaten
25 g/1 oz/2 tbsp butter, melted
SAUCE
1 large, red pepper, chopped
1 small red onion, chopped
30 ml/2 tbsp olive oil
1 × 400 g/14 oz can chopped tomatoes
150 ml/¼ pint/⅔ cup water
good pinch dried oregano
salt and ground black pepper
30 ml/2 tbsp single cream

1 Blanch the spinach in the tiniest amount of water until it is limp, then drain well, pressing it through a sieve with the back of a ladle or spoon. Chop very finely.

COOK'S TIP

Quenelles are oval-shaped dumplings. To shape the Malfatti into quenelles you need two dessertspoons. Scoop up the mixture with one spoon, making sure it is mounded up, then, using the other spoon, scoop the mixture off the first spoon, twisting the top spoon into the bowl of the second.

Repeat this action two or three times until the quenelle is smooth, and then gently knock it off onto a plate ready to cook.

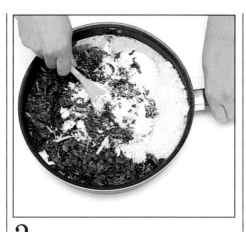

2 Lightly fry the onion and garlic in the oil for 5 minutes then mix with the spinach together with the ricotta, breadcrumbs, flour, salt, most of the Parmesan and nutmeg.

3 Allow the mixture to cool, add the eggs and melted butter, then mould into 12 small 'sausage' shapes.

4 Meanwhile, make the sauce by lightly sautéeing the pepper and onion in the oil for 5 minutes. Add the tomatoes, water, oregano and seasoning. Bring to a boil, then simmer for 5 minutes.

5 When cooked, remove from the heat and blend to a purée in a food processor. Return to the pan, then stir in the cream. Check the seasoning.

6 Bring a shallow pan of salted water to a gentle boil and drop the malfatti into it a few at a time and poach them for about 5 minutes. Drain them well and keep them warm.

7 Arrange the malfatti on warm plates and drizzle over the sauce. Serve topped with the remaining Parmesan.

Curried Mango Chutney Dip

A quickly made, tangy and spicy dip or dressing, ideal as a dip for strips of pitta bread, grissini or sticks of fresh chopped vegetables.

SERVES 4–6
1 onion, chopped
1 garlic clove, crushed
30 ml/2 tbsp sunflower oil
10 ml/2 tsp mild curry powder
225 g/8 oz natural Greek yogurt
30 ml/2 tbsp mango chutney
salt and ground black pepper
30 ml/2 tbsp fresh parsley, chopped

1 Gently fry the onion and garlic in the oil for 5 minutes until they are soft. Add the curry powder and cook for a further minute then allow the mixture to cool.

2 Spoon into a food processor with the yogurt, chutney and seasoning and blend until smooth.

3 Stir in the parsley and chill before serving with a variety of vegetable crudités and strips of bread.

Nutty Mushroom Paté

Spread this delicious, medium-texture paté on chunks of crusty French bread and eat with crisp leaves of lettuce and sweet cherry tomatoes.

SERVES 4–6
1 onion, chopped
1 garlic clove, crushed
15 ml/1 tbsp sunflower oil
30 ml/2 tbsp water
15 ml/1 tbsp dry sherry
225 g/8 oz button mushrooms, chopped
salt and ground black pepper
75 g/3 oz/¾ cup cashew nuts or walnuts, chopped
150 g/5 oz low fat soft cheese
15 ml/1 tbsp soy sauce
few dashes Worcestershire sauce
fresh parsley, chopped, and a little paprika, to serve

1 Gently fry the onion and garlic in the oil for 3 minutes then add the water, sherry and mushrooms. Cook, stirring for about 5 minutes. Season to taste and allow to cool a little.

2 Put the mixture into a food processor with the nuts, cheese and sauces. Blend to a rough purée – do not allow it to become too smooth.

3 Check the seasoning then spoon into a serving dish. Swirl the top and serve lightly chilled sprinkled with parsley and paprika.

Antipasti with Aioli

For a simple starter or hand-around cocktail canapé, make a bowl of the classic French/Spanish garlic sauce – aioli – and serve it with a selection of attractively prepared vegetables and breads.

SERVES 4–6
4 garlic cloves
2 egg yolks
2.5 ml/½ tsp salt
ground black pepper
300 ml/½ pint/1¼ cups extra virgin
   olive oil
TO SERVE
red or yellow pepper, cut in thick strips
fennel, cut in slivers
radishes, halved if large
button mushrooms
broccoli florets
grissini sticks
French bread, thinly sliced

1 Crush the garlic into a bowl then beat in the egg yolks, salt and some ground black pepper.

2 Stand the bowl on a damp cloth and slowly trickle in the oil, drip by drip, whisking with a balloon whisk until you have a thick, creamy sauce. As the sauce thickens, you can add the oil in slightly larger amounts.

3 Spoon the aioli into a bowl. Arrange the dipping food around the bowl and serve lightly chilled.

Camembert Fritters

A popular starter or savoury course at the end of a leisurely dinner. These deep-fried cheeses are quite simple to do. They are served with a red onion marmalade which can be made in advance and stored in the refrigerator.

SERVES 4
MARMALADE
1 kg/2 lb red onions, sliced
45 ml/3 tbsp sunflower oil
45 ml/3 tbsp olive oil
15 ml/1 tbsp coriander berries, crushed
2 large bay leaves
45 ml/3 tbsp granulated sugar
90 ml/6 tbsp red wine vinegar
10 ml/2 tsp salt
CHEESE
8 individual portions of Camembert
1 egg, beaten
125 g/4 oz/1 cup natural colour dried
   breadcrumbs, to coat
oil, for deep fat frying

1 Make the marmalade first. In a large saucepan, gently fry the onions in the oil, covered, for 20 minutes or so or until they are soft.

2 Add the remaining marmalade ingredients, stir well and cook uncovered for a further 10–15 minutes until most of the liquid has been absorbed. Cool and then set aside.

VARIATION

You could make these fritters with fingers of firm Brie, or try it using baby goats' cheese.

3 Prepare the cheese by first scratching the mould rind lightly with a fork. Dip first in egg then in breadcrumbs to coat well. Dip and coat a second time if necessary. Store on a plate.

4 Pour oil into a deep fat fryer so it is one-third full; heat to 190°C/375°F.

5 Carefully lower the coated cheeses into the hot oil three or four at a time and fry until golden and crisp, about 2 minutes or less.

6 Drain well on kitchen paper and fry the rest, reheating the oil in between. Serve hot with some of the marmalade.

DESSERTS & BAKES

Freshly baked breads, cakes and fruit-filled desserts are all utterly irresistible. Here you can also find traditional treats to make Christmas extra special.

Courgette Crown Bread

Adding grated courgettes and cheese to a loaf mixture will keep it tasting fresher for longer. This is a good loaf to serve with a bowl of special soup.

SERVES 8
450 g/1 lb courgettes, coarsely grated
salt
500 g/1¼ lbs/5 cups plain flour
2 sachets fast-action yeast
60 ml/4 tbsp Parmesan cheese, freshly grated
ground black pepper
30 ml/2 tbsp olive oil
lukewarm water, to mix
milk, to glaze
sesame seeds, to garnish

1 Layer the courgettes in a colander and sprinkle them lightly with salt. Leave to drain for 30 minutes, then pat dry.

2 Mix the flour, yeast and Parmesan together and season with black pepper.

3 Stir in the oil and courgettes and add enough lukewarm water to give you a good firm dough.

4 Knead the dough on a lightly floured surface until it is smooth, then return it to the mixing bowl, cover it with oiled cling film and leave it to rise in a warm place.

5 Meanwhile, grease and line a 23 cm/ 9 in round sandwich tin. Preheat the oven to 200°C/400°F/Gas 6.

6 When the dough has doubled in size, turn it out of the bowl, punch it down and knead it lightly. Break into eight balls, rolling each one and placing them in the tin as shown. Brush the tops with milk and sprinkle over the sesame seeds.

7 Allow to rise again, then bake for 25 minutes or until golden brown. Cool slightly in the tin, then turn out the bread to cool further.

Rosemary Focaccia

Italian flat bread is becoming increasingly popular and very easy to make using packet bread mix. Add traditional ingredients like olives and sun-dried tomatoes.

SERVES 4
450 g/1 lb pack white bread mix
60 ml/4 tbsp extra virgin olive oil
10 ml/2 tsp dried rosemary, crushed
8 sun-dried tomatoes, snipped
12 black olives, stoned and chopped
200 ml/7 fl oz/¾ cup lukewarm water
sea salt flakes

VARIATION

If you want to make your own bread instead of using a bread mix, then use a sachet of easy-blend yeast for each 675 g/1½ lbs/6 cups of flour. Mix the yeast and flour together then add the remaining ingredients as per the recipe.

1 Mix the bread mix with half the oil, the rosemary, tomatoes, olives and water until it forms a firm dough.

2 Turn out the dough onto a lightly floured surface and knead thoroughly for 5 minutes. Return the dough to the mixing bowl and cover with a piece of oiled cling film.

3 Leave the dough to rise in a warm place until it has doubled in size. Meanwhile, lightly grease two baking sheets and preheat the oven to 220°C/ 425°F/Gas 7.

4 Turn out the risen dough, punch down and knead again. Divide into two and shape into rounds. Place on the baking sheet, and punch hollows in the dough. Trickle over the remaining olive oil and sprinkle with salt.

5 Bake the focaccia for 12–15 minutes until golden brown and cooked. Slide off onto wire racks to cool. Eat slightly warm.

Brown Soda Bread

This is very easy to make -- simply mix and bake. Instead of yeast, bicarbonate of soda and cream of tartar are the raising agents. This is an excellent recipe for those new to bread making.

MAKES ONE 1 KG/2 LB LOAF
450 g/1 lb/4 cups plain flour
450 g/1 lb/3 cups wholemeal flour
10 ml/2 tsp salt
15 ml/1 tbsp bicarbonate of soda
20 ml/4 tsp cream of tartar
10 ml/2 tsp caster sugar
50 g/2 oz/4 tbsp butter
up to 900 ml/1½ pints/3¾ cups buttermilk or skimmed milk
extra wholemeal flour, to sprinkle

1 Lightly grease a baking sheet. Preheat the oven to 190°C/375°F/Gas 5.

2 Sift all the dry ingredients into a large bowl, tipping any bran from the flour back into the bowl.

3 Rub the butter into the flour mixture, then add enough buttermilk or milk to make a soft dough. You may not need all of it, so add it cautiously.

4 Knead lightly until smooth then transfer to the baking sheet and shape to a large round about 5 cm/2 in thick.

5 Using the floured handle of a wooden spoon, form a large cross on top of the dough. Sprinkle over a little extra wholemeal flour.

6 Bake for 40–50 minutes until risen and firm. Cool for 5 minutes before transferring to a wire rack to cool further.

Cardamom and Saffron Tea Loaf

An aromatic sweet bread ideal for afternoon tea, or lightly toasted for breakfast. Use the sachets of fast action or easy blend yeasts, they make bread making so simple.

MAKES ONE 1 KG/2 LB LOAF
good pinch saffron strands
750 ml/1¼ pints/3 cups lukewarm milk
25 g/1 oz/2 tbsp butter
1 kg/2 lb/8 cups strong plain flour
2 sachets fast action yeast
30 g/1½ oz caster sugar
6 cardamom pods, split open and seeds extracted
115 g/4 oz/⅔ cup raisins
30 ml/2 tbsp clear honey
1 egg, beaten

1 Crush the saffron into a cup containing a little of the warm milk and leave to infuse for 5 minutes.

2 Rub the butter into the flour then mix in the yeast, sugar and cardamom seeds (these may need rubbing to separate them). Stir in the raisins.

3 Beat the remaining milk with the honey and egg, then mix this into the flour along with the saffron milk and strands, stirring well until a firm dough is formed. You may not need all the milk: it depends on the flour.

4 Turn out the dough and knead it on a lightly floured board for about 5 minutes until smooth.

5 Return the dough to the mixing bowl, cover with oiled cling film and leave in a warm place until doubled in size. This could take between 1–3 hours.

VARIATION

For simplicity, leave out the saffron and cardamom and add 10 ml/2 tsp ground cinnamon.

6 Turn the dough out onto a floured board again, punch it down, knead for 3 minutes then shape it into a fat roll and fit it into a greased loaf tin.

7 Cover with a sheet of lightly oiled cling film and stand in a warm place until the dough begins to rise again. Preheat the oven to 200°C/400°F/Gas 6.

8 Bake the loaf for 25 minutes until golden brown and firm on top. Turn out of the tin and as it cools brush the top with honey. Slice when cold and spread with butter. It is also good lightly toasted.

Dinner Milk Rolls

Making bread especially for your dinner guests is not only a wonderful gesture, it is also quite easy to do. You can vary the shapes of the rolls too.

MAKES 12–16
750 g/1½ lb/4 cups strong plain flour
10 ml/2 tsp salt
25 g/1 oz/2 tbsp butter
1 sachet easy-blend fast action yeast
about 450 ml/¾ pint/scant 2 cups lukewarm milk
extra cold milk, to glaze
poppy, sesame and sunflower seeds or sea salt flakes, to garnish

1 Sift the flour and salt into a large bowl or food processor. Rub in the butter, then mix in the yeast.

2 Mix to a firm dough with the milk, adding it cautiously if the dough is a little dry in case you don't need it all.

3 Knead for at least 5 minutes by hand, or for 2 minutes in a food processor. Place in a bowl, cover with oiled cling film and leave to rise until doubled in size.

4 Turn out of the bowl, punch down and knead again, then break off into 12–16 pieces and either roll each one into a round or make into fun shapes.

5 Place on an oiled baking sheet, glaze the tops with extra milk and sprinkle over seeds or sea salt flakes of your choice.

6 Leave to start rising again, while you preheat the oven to 230°C/450°F/Gas 8. Bake the rolls for 12 minutes or until golden brown and cooked. Cool on a wire rack. Eat the same day, as homemade bread stales quickly.

Indian Pan-fried Breads

Instead of yeast, this dough uses bicarbonate of soda as a raising agent. Traditional Indian spices add a tasty bite to the bread.

MAKES ABOUT 24
250 g/8 oz/2 cups wholemeal flour
250 g/8 oz/2 cups plain flour
5 ml/1 tsp salt
5 ml/1 tsp sugar
10 ml/2 tsp bicarbonate of soda
10 ml/2 tsp cumin seeds
10 ml/2 tsp black mustard seeds
5 ml/1 tsp fennel seeds
450 g/1 lb natural yogurt
75 g/3 oz/6 tbsp vegetable ghee or clarified butter
75 ml/5 tbsp sunflower oil

1 Mix the flours with the salt, sugar, bicarbonate of soda and spices. Mix to a firm dough with the yogurt. Be sure to add the yogurt gradually, as you may not need it all.

2 If the dough is too dry, add cold water slowly until you achieve the correct consistency. Cover and chill for 2 hours.

3 Divide the dough into 24 pieces and roll each piece out to a thin round. Stack the rounds under a clean tea towel as you roll out the rest.

4 Fry the breads in the hot ghee or butter and oil, starting with a quarter and adding more ghee/butter and oil each time you fry. Drain the breads well on kitchen paper towel and store under the tea towel. Serve with curries and raitas.

Rich Chocolate Cake

A simple all-in-one cake sandwiched with a simple but very delicious ganache icing. It makes a particularly good special-occasion cake.

SERVES 6–8
115 g/4 oz/1 cup self-raising flour
25 g/1 oz/3 tbsp cocoa
5 ml/1 tsp baking powder
120 g/5 oz/10 tbsp butter, softened, or sunflower margarine
120 g/5 oz/¾ cup caster sugar
3 eggs, beaten
30 ml/2 tbsp water
ICING
150 g/5 oz dark (plain) chocolate
150 ml/¼ pint/⅔ cup double cream
5 ml/1 tsp vanilla essence
30 ml/2 tbsp apricot or raspberry jam

1 Grease and line a deep 20 cm/8 in round cake tin. Preheat the oven to 160°C/325°F/Gas 3.

2 Put all the cake ingredients into a large bowl or food processor. Beat very well with a wooden spoon or blend in a food processor until the mixture is smooth and creamy.

3 Spoon into the cake tin and bake for about 40–45 minutes or until risen and springy to the touch. Cool upside down on a wire rack for 15 minutes, then turn out and set aside to cool completely.

4 To make the icing, break the chocolate into a heatproof bowl and pour in the cream and vanilla essence. Melt in a microwave on full power for 2–3 minutes, or over a pan of simmering water.

5 Cool the icing, stirring it occasionally and chill lightly until it thickens. Split the cake in half. Spread the jam on one half and half the icing on top of that.

6 Sandwich the two halves together and spread the rest of the icing on top, swirling it attractively or marking it with the tip of a table knife. Decorate as desired with candies or candles – even edible flowers can add a nice touch.

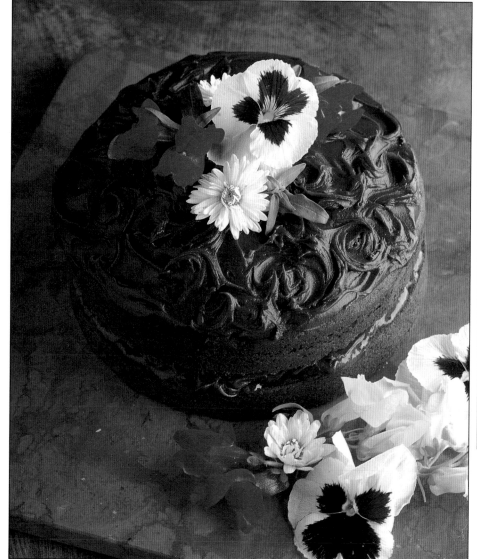

Passion Cake

So called because this is a cake associated with Passion Sunday. The carrot and banana give the cake a rich, moist texture.

SERVES 6–8
200 g/7 oz/1¾ cups self-raising flour
10 ml/2 tsp baking powder
5 ml/1 tsp cinnamon
2.5 ml/½ tsp fresh nutmeg, grated
120 g/5 oz/10 tbsp butter, softened, or
  sunflower margarine
120 g/5 oz/¾ cup soft brown sugar
grated rind of 1 lemon
2 eggs, beaten
2 carrots, coarsely grated
1 ripe banana, mashed
115 g/4 oz/¾ cup raisins
50 g/2 oz/½ cup walnuts or pecans,
  chopped
30 ml/2 tbsp milk
FROSTING
200 g/7 oz cream cheese, softened
30 g/1½ oz icing sugar
juice of 1 lemon
grated rind of 1 orange
6–8 walnuts, halved
coffee crystal sugar, to sprinkle

1 Line and grease a deep 20 cm/8 in cake tin. Preheat the oven to 180°C/350°F/ Gas 4. Sift the flour, baking powder and spices into a bowl.

2 Using an electric mixer, cream the butter and sugar with the lemon rind until it is light and fluffy, then beat in the eggs. Fold in the flour mixture, then the carrots, banana, raisins, nuts and milk.

3 Spoon the mixture into the prepared tin, level the top and bake for about 1 hour until it is risen and the top is springy to touch. Turn the tin upside down and allow the cake to cool in the tin for 30 minutes. Turn onto a wire rack.

4 When cold, split the cake in half. Cream the cheese with the icing sugar, lemon juice and orange rind, then sandwich the two halves together with half of the frosting.

5 Spread the rest of the frosting on top, swirling it attractively. Decorate with the walnut halves and sprinkle with the coffee crystal sugar.

Yogurt with Apricots and Pistachios

If you allow a thick yogurt to drain overnight, it becomes even thicker and more luscious. Add honeyed apricots and nuts and you have an exotic yet simple dessert.

SERVES 4
450 g/1 lb Greek-style yogurt
175 g/6 oz/⅔ cup no-need-to-soak dried apricots, snipped
15 ml/1 tbsp clear honey
orange rind, grated
30 ml/2 tbsp unsalted pistachios, roughly chopped
ground cinnamon

VARIATION

For a simple dessert, strain the fruit, cover with yogurt and sprinkle with demerara sugar and a little mixed spice or cinnamon.

1 Place the yogurt in a fine sieve and allow it to drain overnight in the fridge over a bowl.

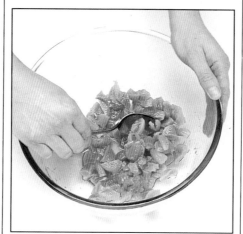

2 Discard the whey from the yogurt. Place the apricots in a saucepan, barely cover with water and simmer for just 3 minutes, to soften. Drain and cool, then mix with the honey.

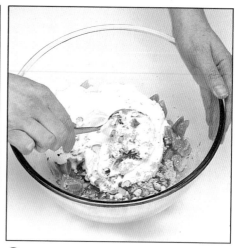

3 Mix the yogurt with the apricots, orange rind and nuts. Spoon into sundae dishes, sprinkle over a little cinnamon and chill.

Fresh Pineapple Salad

Very refreshing, this salad can be prepared ahead. Orange flower water is available from Middle Eastern food stores or good delicatessens.

SERVES 4
1 small ripe pineapple
icing sugar, to taste
15 ml/1 tbsp orange flower water, or more if liked
115 g/4 oz/good ½ cup fresh dates, stoned and quartered
225 g/8 oz fresh strawberries, sliced
few fresh mint sprigs, to serve

1 Cut the skin from the pineapple and, using the tip of a vegetable peeler, remove as many brown 'eyes' as possible. Quarter lengthways, remove the core then slice.

2 Lay the pineapple in a shallow, pretty, glass bowl. Sprinkle with sugar and orange flower water.

3 Add the dates and strawberries to the pineapple, cover and chill for a good 2 hours, stirring once or twice. Serve lightly chilled decorated with a few mint sprigs.

Walnut and Raspberry Meringue

Make sure you beat the egg whites stiffly to form a good firm foam for the meringue. When you fold in the nuts the meringue will hold its shape. Assemble this dish just before serving, if at all possible.

SERVES 4–6
3 egg whites
few drops of fresh lemon juice
175 g/6 oz/1 cup caster sugar
75 g/3 oz/¾ cup walnuts, finely chopped
450 g/1 lb fresh raspberries
200 ml/7 fl oz/¾ cup crème fraîche or
  double cream
few drops vanilla essence
icing sugar, to taste

1 Preheat the oven to 160°C/325°F/ Gas 3. Draw three 20 cm/8 in circles on non-stick baking parchment. Place the circles on baking sheets.

COOK'S TIP

Don't waste egg whites if you have recipes which call for yolks only. They do freeze very well and can be stored in batches of 3 or 4 whites at a time. In fact, when thawed, frozen egg whites make a much better foam.

2 Whisk the egg whites in a spotlessly clean and grease-free bowl with the few drops of lemon juice. (This gives a more stable foam).

3 When the whites are softly stiff, gradually whisk in the sugar until thick and glossy. Quickly and carefully fold in the nuts.

4 Spread or pipe the mixture onto the three paper circles. Bake for 40–50 minutes until firm and crisp on top. This may have to be done in batches.

5 Cool on a wire rack and peel off the paper. Store in an airtight container until ready to serve.

6 Whip the crème fraîche or cream with the vanilla and sugar, until the mixture is quite stiff.

7 Reserve a few raspberries for decoration, crush those remaining and mix into the creamy cheese mixture.

8 Spread the fruit cream on the three meringues. Sandwich them together and decorate the top layer with the reserved raspberries.

Rum-Baked Bananas

This is a quick, hot pudding which bakes in just minutes. When cooked, bananas have a really full flavour that is enhanced by rum and orange. Serve this dish with a trickle of cream.

SERVES 4
4 bananas
grated rind and juice of 1 orange
30 ml/2 tbsp dark rum
50 g/2 oz/¼ cup soft brown sugar
  (optional)
good pinch of ground ginger
fresh nutmeg, grated
40 g/1½ oz/3 tbsp butter

1 Preheat the oven to 180°C/350°F/ Gas 4. Peel the bananas and slice them into four large ramekins.

2 Spoon the orange juice and rum over the sliced bananas. Sprinkle over the sugar, if using, orange rind and spices. Dot with butter.

3 Cover the ramekins with small pieces of foil or buttered papers and bake for 15 minutes. Allow to cool slightly before serving with cream or natural yogurt.

Muesli Bars

Instead of buying expensive crunchy oat bars, bake your own. They are much nicer and really quite easy to make. Use muesli with no added sugar for the bars.

MAKES 12–16
350 g/12 oz/4 cups muesli
75 ml/5 tbsp sunflower oil
75 ml/5 tbsp clear honey
5 ml/1 tsp mixed spice
1 egg, beaten
30 g/1½ oz molasses sugar (optional)

COOK'S TIP

To make your own muesli, buy bags of flaked grains and oats from your local health food store. As these will make a large amount, you need to make sure you eat a lot of muesli! Choose jumbo porridge oats, barley flakes and wheat flakes, then add seeds, dried fruits and nuts of your choice.

1 Preheat the oven to 160°C/325°F/ Gas 3. Grease and line a shallow baking tin about 18 × 28 cm/7 × 11 in.

2 Mix all the ingredients together and spoon into the tin, patting the mixture until it is level.

3 Bake for 30–35 minutes until light brown round the edges. Remove, cool slightly then mark into 12–16 pieces.

4 Cool completely, turn out onto a wire rack and break into the marked pieces. Store in an airtight tin.

Oatmeal and Date Brownies

These brownies are marvellous for special brunches or as a tea time treat. The secret of chewy, moist brownies is not to overcook them.

MAKES 16

150 g/5 oz dark (plain) chocolate
50 g/2 oz/4 tbsp butter
75 g/3 oz/¾ cup quick-cook porridge oats
25 g/1 oz/3 tbsp wheat germ
25 g/1 oz/⅓ cup milk powder
2.5 ml/½ tsp baking powder
2.5 ml/½ tsp salt
50 g/2 oz/½ cup walnuts, chopped
50 g/2 oz/⅓ cup dates, chopped
50 g/2 oz/¼ cup molasses sugar
5 ml/1 tsp vanilla essence
2 eggs, beaten

1 Break the chocolate into a heatproof bowl and add the butter. Melt it either in a microwave on full power for 2 minutes, stirring once, or in a pan over very gently simmering water.

2 Cool the chocolate, stirring it occasionally. Grease and line a 20 cm/8 in square cake tin. Preheat the oven to 180°C/350°F/Gas 4.

3 Combine all the dry ingredients together in a bowl then beat in the melted chocolate, vanilla and eggs.

4 Pour the mixture into the prepared cake tin, level the top and bake for about 20–25 minutes until it is firm around the edges yet still soft in the centre.

5 Cool the brownies in the tin then chill them. When they are more solid, turn them out of the tin and cut into 16 squares. Store in an airtight tin.

COOK'S TIP

These make a marvellous lunch box or picnic snack, and if you store them for a day or two before eating they will become more moist and even more chewy.

Cut-and-Come-Again Fruit Cake

A rich fruit cake keeps well for quite some time so it is ideal to have one on hand for when you feel like a slice of something sweet or when guests drop in unexpectedly.

SERVES 8–10
225 g/8 oz/1 cup butter, softened, or
    sunflower margarine
225 g/8 oz/1 cup soft brown sugar
4 eggs, beaten
15 ml/1 tbsp black treacle
350 g/12 oz/3 cups plain flour
5 ml/1 tsp mixed spice
45 ml/3 tbsp milk
900 g/2 lb dried mixed fruit (e.g. raisins,
    currants, cherries)
50 g/2 oz/½ cup flaked almonds
grated rind of 1 lemon
a few blanched almond halves (optional)
a little milk, to glaze (optional)
30 ml/2 tbsp brandy or rum (optional)

1 Preheat the oven to 140°C/275°F/ Gas 1. Grease and line a deep 20 cm/8 in cake tin with doubled greaseproof paper.

2 Cream the butter or margarine and sugar until light and fluffy. Beat in the eggs with the treacle and stir into the creamed mixture.

3 Sift the flour and spice and fold this into the mixture, alternating it with the milk. Stir in the dried fruit, almonds and lemon rind.

4 Spoon the mixture into the prepared tin. If liked, dip the almond halves in a little milk and arrange them on top.

5 Bake on a shelf one position below the centre of the oven for about 3 hours. When cooked, the top of the cake will feel quite firm and a skewer inserted into the centre will come out clean.

6 Allow the cake to cool for 10 minutes then, if using the brandy or rum, make small holes in the top of the cake with a thin skewer. Slowly pour the spirit over the cake.

7 Allow the cake to cool completely in the tin, then turn it out and remove the paper. Wrap it in clean greaseproof paper and foil or store in an airtight container for one week before cutting.

Thai Rice Cake

A celebration gâteau made from fragrant Thai rice covered with a tangy cream icing. Top with fresh berry fruits or pipe on a greeting in melted chocolate. This is a good cake to serve to those with a gluten allergy as it is flour free.

SERVES 8–10
225 g/8 oz/1¼ cups Thai fragrant or
  Jasmine rice
1 litre/1¾ pints/4½ cups milk
115 g/4 oz/¾ cup caster sugar
6 cardamom pods, crushed open
2 bay leaves
300 ml/½ pint/1¼ cups whipping cream
6 eggs, separated
TOPPING
300 ml/½ pint/1¼ cups double cream
200 g/7 oz quark
5 ml/1 tsp vanilla essence
grated rind of 1 lemon
30 g/1½ oz caster sugar
soft berry fruits and sliced star or kiwi
  fruits, to decorate

1 Grease and line a deep 25 cm/10 in round cake tin. Boil the rice in unsalted water for 3 minutes then drain.

2 Return the rice to the pan with the milk, sugar, cardamom and bay leaves. Bring to the boil, then lower the heat and simmer the mixture for 20 minutes, stirring it occasionally.

3 Allow the mixture to cool, then remove the bay leaves and any cardamom husks. Turn into a bowl. Beat in the cream and then the egg yolks. Preheat the oven to 180°C/350°F/Gas 4.

VARIATION

If you prefer something simpler, turn the cake out and top with sliced fruits or a lovely tumble of berries and stoned cherries. Serve the topping separately, thinning it down slightly with a little milk.

4 Whisk the egg whites until they are softly stiff and fold into the rice mixture. Spoon into the prepared tin and bake for 45–50 minutes until risen and golden brown. The centre should be slightly wobbly – it will firm up as it cools.

5 Chill overnight in the tin. Turn out on to a large serving plate. Whip the double cream until stiff then mix in the quark, vanilla essence, lemon rind and sugar.

6 Cover the top and sides of the cake with the cream, swirling it attractively. Decorate with soft berry fruits and sliced star or kiwi fruits.

Apple and Apricot Crumble

Lightly cook the fruit base first for the best results. That way you'll get a delicious contrast between soft fruit and crunchy topping.

SERVES 4–6
1 × 425 g/15 oz can apricot halves in natural juice
450 g/1 lb cooking apples, peeled and sliced
granulated sugar, to taste (optional)
grated rind of 1 orange
fresh nutmeg, grated
TOPPING
200 g/7 oz/1¾ cups plain flour
50 g/2 oz/½ cup rolled porridge oats
120 g/5 oz/10 tbsp butter or sunflower margarine
50 g/2 oz/¼ cup soft brown sugar
demerara sugar, to sprinkle

1 Preheat the oven to 190°C/375°F/ Gas 5. Drain the apricots, reserving a little of the juice.

2 Put the apples into a saucepan with a little of the reserved apricot juice and sugar to taste. Simmer for just 5 minutes to cook the fruit lightly.

3 Transfer the apples into an ovenproof pie dish and stir in the apricots, orange rind and nutmeg to taste.

4 Rub the flour, oats and butter or margarine together until they form fine crumbs. (You can use a food processor if you prefer.) Mix in the soft brown sugar.

5 Scatter the crumble over the fruit, spreading it evenly. Sprinkle with a little demerara sugar. Bake for about 30 minutes until golden and crisp on top. Allow to cool slightly before serving.

French Apple Cake

With its moist texture and fruity flavour, this cake is ideal to serve as a dessert accompanied by a little cream or fromage frais.

SERVES 6–8
450 g/1 lb cooking apples or tart dessert
   apples, cored and chopped
115 g/4 oz/1 cup self-raising flour
5 ml/1 tsp baking powder
115 g/4 oz/⅔ cup caster sugar
90 ml/6 tbsp milk
50 g/2 oz/4 tbsp butter, melted
3 eggs
5 ml/1 tsp fresh nutmeg, grated
TOPPING
75 g/3 oz/6 tbsp butter, softened, or
   sunflower margarine
115 g/4 oz/½ cup caster sugar
5 ml/1 tsp vanilla essence
sifted icing sugar, to dust

1 Preheat the oven to 160°C/325°F/ Gas 3. Grease and line the base of a deep 23 cm/9 in round cake tin.

2 Put the chopped apples into the base of the cake tin.

3 Put all the remaining cake ingredients, except 1 egg, into a bowl or food processor. Beat to a smooth batter.

4 Pour the batter over the apples in the tin, level the top then bake for 40–45 minutes until lightly golden.

5 Meanwhile, cream the topping ingredients together with the remaining egg. Remove the cake from the oven and spoon over the topping.

6 Return the cake to the oven for a further 20–25 minutes until it is golden brown. Cool the cake in the tin, then turn it out and finish with a light dusting of icing sugar.

VARIATION

We don't use fresh fruit very often in cake mixtures, which is a pity as it gives a delightful flavour. Try adding finely chopped pears or pineapple, or even raspberries.

Chocolate and Lemon Fromage Frais

What better excuse to add iron to your diet than by eating some good dark (plain) chocolate? Contrast the richness with tangy fromage frais.

SERVES 4
120 g/5 oz dark (plain) chocolate
45 ml/3 tbsp water
15 ml/1 tbsp rum, brandy or whisky (optional)
grated rind of 1 lemon
200 g/7 oz low fat fromage frais
TO DECORATE
kumquats, sliced
sprigs of mint

COOK'S TIP

If you heat chocolate too quickly or fiercely, the cocoa solids will 'seize' and go lumpy and nothing can then be done to make a smooth all-chocolate sauce.

1 Break up the chocolate into a heatproof bowl. Add the water and either melt very slowly over a pan of gently simmering water or in a microwave on full power for 2–2½ minutes.

2 Stir well until smooth and allow the chocolate to cool for 10 minutes. Stir in the spirit, if using, and the lemon rind and fromage frais.

3 Spoon into four elegant wine glasses and chill until set. Decorate with kumquats and sprigs of mint.

Orange, Honey and Mint Terrine 🍃

Very refreshing and easy to make, this is an ideal dessert to serve after a rich meal as it is a good palate cleanser.

SERVES 6
8–10 oranges
600 ml/1 pint/2½ cups fresh orange juice
30 ml/2 tbsp clear honey
20 ml/4 tsp agar-agar
45 ml/3 tbsp fresh mint, chopped
mint leaves to decorate (optional)

1 Grate the rind from two oranges and put this aside. Cut the peel and membrane from all the oranges, then slice each one thinly, removing any pips, and saving any juice.

2 Heat the orange juice (plus any saved) with the honey, reserved rind and agar-agar. Stir the mixture until it dissolves.

3 Pack the orange slices into a 1 kg/2 lb loaf tin, sprinkling the mint in between. Slowly pour over the hot orange juice. Tap the tin lightly so that all the juice settles.

4 Chill the terrine overnight, if possible, until it is quite firm. When ready to serve, dip the tin briefly into very hot water and turn the terrine out to a wet platter. Decorate with more mint leaves, if you wish. Serve cut into thick slices.

Halva

The Greeks love homemade halva which they cook in a saucepan with semolina, olive oil, sugar, honey and almonds. You can either eat it warm, or allow it to set and cut it into slices or squares.

MAKES 12–16 PIECES
400 g/14 oz/2 cups granulated sugar
1 litre/1¾ pints/4½ cups water
2 cinnamon sticks
225 ml/8 fl oz/1 cup olive oil
350 g/12 oz/3 cups semolina
75 g/3 oz/¾ cup blanched almonds, 6–8 halved, the rest chopped
120 ml/4 fl oz/½ cup clear honey
ground cinnamon, to serve

1 Reserve 60 ml/4 tbsp sugar and dissolve the rest in the water over a gentle heat, stirring from time to time.

2 Add the cinnamon sticks, bring to a boil then simmer for 5 minutes. Cool and remove the cinnamon sticks.

3 Heat the olive oil in a large heavy-based saucepan and, when it is quite hot, stir in the semolina. Cook, stirring occasionally, until it turns a golden brown, then add the chopped almonds and cook for a further minute or so.

4 Keep the heat low and stir in the syrup, taking care as the semolina may spit. Bring the mixture to a boil, stirring it constantly. When it is just smooth, remove the pan from the heat and stir in the honey.

5 Cool slightly and mix in the reserved sugar. Pour the halva into a greased and lined shallow tin, pat it down and mark into squares.

6 Sprinkle the halva lightly with ground cinnamon and fix one almond half on each square. When set, cut up and serve.

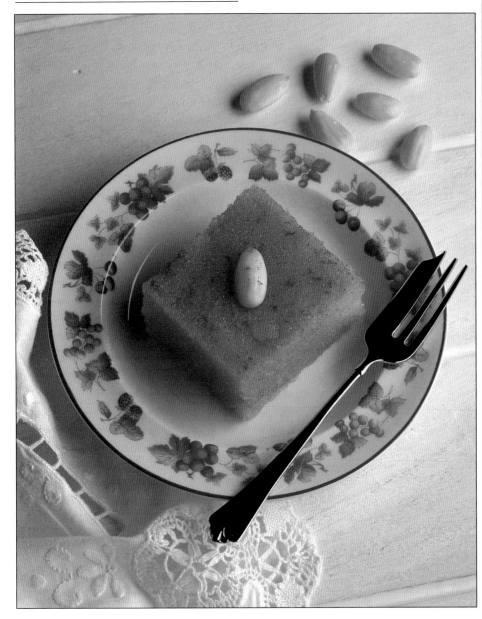

Rice Condé Sundae

Cook a rice pudding on top of the stove instead of in the oven for a light creamy texture which is particularly good served cold topped with fruits, toasted nuts and even a trickle of hot chocolate sauce.

SERVES 4
50 g/2 oz/⅓ cup pudding rice
600 ml/1 pint/2½ cups milk
5ml/1 tsp vanilla essence
2.5 ml/½ tsp ground cinnamon
30 g/1½ oz granulated sugar
TO SERVE
Choose from: strawberries, raspberries or blueberries
chocolate sauce
flaked toasted almonds

1 Put the rice, milk, vanilla essence, cinnamon and sugar into a medium-sized saucepan. Bring to the boil, stirring constantly, and then turn down the heat to a gentle simmer.

2 Cook the rice for about 30–40 minutes, stirring occasionally. Add extra milk if it reduces down too quickly.

3 Make sure the grains are soft, then remove the pan from the heat and allow the rice to cool, stirring it occasionally. When cold, chill the rice in the refrigerator.

4 Just before serving, stir the rice and spoon into four sundae dishes. Top with fruits, chocolate sauce and almonds.

VARIATION

Milk puddings are at last enjoying something of a comeback in popularity. Instead of simple pudding rice try using a Thai fragrant or Jasmine rice for a delicious natural flavour. For a firmer texture, an Italian Arborio rice makes a good pudding too.

There's no need to use a lot of high-fat milk or cream either. A pudding made with semi-skimmed or even fat-free milk can be just as nice and is much more healthy.

Pear and Hazelnut Flan

A delicious flan for Sunday lunch. Ground hazelnuts are increasingly easier to find, but if you have difficulty, then either grind your own or use ground almonds instead.

SERVES 6–8
115 g/4 oz/1 cup plain flour
115 g/4 oz/¾ cup wholemeal flour
about 45 ml/3 tbsp cold water
115 g/4 oz/8 tbsp sunflower margarine
FILLING
50 g/2 oz/½ cup self-raising flour
115 g/4 oz/1 cup ground hazelnuts
5 ml/1 tsp vanilla essence
50 g/2 oz caster sugar
50 g/2 oz/4 tbsp butter, softened
2 eggs, beaten
45 ml/3 tbsp raspberry jam
1 × 400 g/14 oz can pears in natural juice
a few chopped hazelnuts, to decorate

1 Stir the flours together in a large mixing bowl, then rub in the margarine until it resembles fine crumbs. Mix to a firm dough with the water.

2 Roll out the pastry and use it to line a 23–5 cm/9–10 in flan tin, pressing it firmly up the sides after trimming, so the pastry sits above the tin a little. Prick the base, line with greaseproof paper and fill with baking beans. Chill for 30 minutes.

3 Preheat the oven to 200°C/400°F/Gas 6. Place the flan tin on a baking sheet and bake blind for 20 minutes, removing the paper and beans for the last 5 minutes.

4 Meanwhile, beat all the filling ingredients together except for the jam and pears. If the mixture is a little thick, stir in some of the pear juice.

5 Reduce the oven temperature to 180°C/350°F/Gas 4. Spread the jam on the pastry base and spoon over the filling.

6 Drain the pears well and arrange them cut side down in the filling. Scatter over the nuts and bake for 30 minutes until risen, firm and golden brown.

VARIATION

This is also good made with ground almonds and canned apricots or pineapple pieces. For chocaholics, add 30 ml/2 tbsp of cocoa powder to the flour in the filling (and even to the pastry if you want to make it richer and more chocolatey) plus a little grated lemon rind. Instead of raspberry jam, you could use chocolate spread and top with the pears in the recipe.

Three-fruits Compôte

Mixing dried fruits with fresh ones makes a good combination, especially if flavoured delicately with a little orange flower water. A melon-ball scoop gives the compôte a classy touch, but you could chop the melon into cubes.

SERVES 6

175 g/6 oz/1 cup dried, no-need-to-soak apricots
1 small ripe pineapple
1 small ripe melon
15 ml/1 tbsp orange flower water

1 Put the apricots into a saucepan with 300 ml/½ pint water. Bring to the boil, then simmer for 5 minutes. Leave to cool.

2 Peel and quarter the pineapple then cut the core from each quarter and discard. Cut the flesh into chunks.

3 Seed the melon and scoop balls from the flesh. Save any juices which fall from the fruits and tip them into the apricots.

4 Stir in the orange flower water and mix all the fruits together. Pour into an attractive serving dish and chill lightly before serving.

VARIATION

A good fruit salad needn't be a boring mixture of multi-coloured fruits swimming in sweet syrup. Instead of the usual apple, orange and grape type of salad, give it a theme, such as red berry fruits or a variety of sliced green fruits – even a dish of just one fruit nicely prepared and sprinkled lightly with some sugar and fresh lemon juice can look beautiful and tastes delicious. Do not use more than three fruits in a salad so that the flavours remain distinct.

Red Berry Tart with Lemon Cream Filling

Just right for warm summer days, this flan is best filled just before serving so the pastry remains mouth-wateringly crisp. Select red berry fruits such as strawberries, raspberries or redcurrants.

SERVES 6–8
150 g/5 oz/1¼ cups plain flour
25 g/1 oz/¼ cup cornflour
30 g/1½ oz icing sugar
100 g/3½ oz/8 tbsp butter
5 ml/1 tsp vanilla essence
2 egg yolks, beaten
FILLING
200 g/7 oz cream cheese, softened
45 ml/3 tbsp lemon curd
grated rind and juice of 1 lemon
icing sugar, to sweeten (optional)
225 g/8 oz mixed red berry fruits
45 ml/3 tbsp redcurrant jelly

1 Sift the flour, cornflour and icing sugar together, then rub in the butter until the mixture resembles breadcrumbs. This can be done in a food processor.

2 Beat the vanilla into the egg yolks, then mix into the crumbs to make a firm dough, adding cold water if necessary.

3 Roll out and line a 23 cm/9 in round flan tin, pressing the dough well up the sides after trimming. Prick the base of the flan with a fork and allow it to rest in the refrigerator for 30 minutes.

4 Preheat the oven to 200°C/400°F/ Gas 6. Line the flan with greaseproof paper and baking beans. Place the tin on a baking sheet and bake for 20 minutes, removing the paper and beans for the last 5 minutes. When cooked, cool and remove the pastry case from the flan tin.

VARIATION

There are all sorts of delightful variations to this recipe. For instance, leave out the redcurrant jelly and sprinkle lightly with icing sugar or decorate with fresh mint leaves. Alternatively, top with sliced kiwi fruits or bananas.

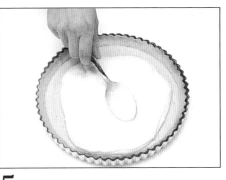

5 Cream the cheese, lemon curd and lemon rind and juice, adding icing sugar to sweeten, if you wish. Spread the mixture into the base of the flan.

6 Top the flan with the fruits. Warm the redcurrant jelly and trickle it over the fruits just before serving.

Avocado and Lime Ice Cream

In some parts of the world, avocadoes are frequently eaten as desserts. In fact, their rich texture makes them perfect for a smooth, creamy and delicious ice cream.

SERVES 4–6
4 egg yolks
300 ml/½ pint/1¼ cups whipping cream
115 g/4 oz/½ cup granulated sugar
2 ripe avocadoes
grated rind of 2 limes
juice of 1 lime
2 egg whites
few unsalted pistachio nuts, to serve

1 Beat the yolks in a heatproof bowl. In a saucepan, heat the cream with the sugar, stirring it well until it dissolves.

2 As the cream rises to the top of the pan at the point of boiling, remove it from the heat.

3 Gently pour the beaten egg yolks into the scalded cream, adding them in small amounts from a height above the saucepan. This stops the mixture from curdling. Allow the mixture to cool, stirring it occasionally, then chill.

COOK'S TIP

If you have an ice cream machine, then simply pour the mixture into the basin and switch on. No need to add the egg whites as air is already beaten in with the paddle.

4 Peel and mash the avocadoes until they are smooth then beat them into the custard with the lime rind and juice. Check for sweetness. Ice cream should be quite sweet before freezing as it loses flavour when ice cold. Add extra sugar now if you think it is needed.

5 Pour the mixture into a shallow container and freeze it until it is slushy. Beat it well once or twice as it freezes to stop large ice crystals forming.

6 Whisk the egg whites until softly stiff and fold into the ice cream. Return the mixture to the freezer and freeze until firm. Cover and label. Use within four weeks, decorated with pistachio nuts.

Honey and Lemon Spicy Mincemeat 🍂

Like Christmas Pudding, mincemeat is best made a few weeks ahead to allow the flavours to mature. This mixture is lighter than most traditional recipes.

MAKES 1.5 KG/3 LB
150 g/6 oz/1 cup vegetarian shredded suet
225 g/8 oz/1½ cups currants
1 large cooking apple, coarsely grated
grated rind of 2 lemons
grated rind and juice of 1 orange
115 g/4 oz/¾ cup no-need-to-soak prunes, chopped
115 g/4 oz/¾ cup stoned dates, chopped
150 g/6 oz/1 cup raisins
225 g/8 oz/1¼ cups sultanas
115 g/4 oz/1 cup flaked almonds
90 ml/6 tbsp clear honey
60 ml/4 tbsp brandy or rum
5 ml/1 tsp mixed spice
2.5 ml/½ tsp ground cloves or all-spice

1 Mix all the ingredients together well in a large mixing bowl. Cover and store in a cool place for two days, stirring the mixture occasionally.

2 Sterilize clean jam jars by placing them in a warm oven for 30 minutes. Cool, then fill with mincemeat, and seal with wax discs and screw tops. Label and store until required.

Cinnamon and Treacle Cookies

The smell of homemade cookies baking is bettered only by their wonderful taste! These cookies are slightly sticky, spicy and nutty.

MAKES 24
30 ml/2 tbsp black treacle
50 g/2 oz/4 tbsp butter or margarine
115 g/4 oz/1 cup plain flour
1.25 ml/¼ tsp bicarbonate of soda
2.5 ml/½ tsp ground ginger
5 ml/1 tsp ground cinnamon
40 g/1½ oz/¼ cup soft brown sugar
15 ml/1 tbsp ground almonds or hazelnuts
1 egg yolk
115 g/4 oz/1 cup icing sugar, sifted

1 Heat the treacle and butter or margarine until it just begins to melt.

2 Sift the flour into a large bowl with the bicarbonate of soda and spices, then stir in the sugar and almonds or nuts.

3 Beat the treacle mixture briskly into the bowl together with the egg yolk and draw the ingredients together to form a firm but soft dough.

4 Roll the dough out on a lightly floured surface to a 5 mm/¼ in thickness and stamp out shapes, such as stars, hearts or circles. Re-roll the trimmings for more shapes. Place on a very lightly greased baking sheet and chill for 15 minutes.

5 Meanwhile, preheat the oven to 190°C/375°F/Gas 5. Prick the cookies lightly with a fork and bake them for 12–15 minutes until just firm. Cool on wire trays to crisp up.

6 To decorate, mix the icing sugar with a little lukewarm water to make it slightly runny, then drizzle it over the biscuits on the wire tray.

Mince Pies with Orange Cinnamon Pastry

Homemade mince pies are so much nicer than shop bought, especially with a flavoursome pastry.

MAKES 18
225 g/8 oz/2 cups plain flour
30 g/1½ oz icing sugar
10 ml/2 tsp ground cinnamon
120 g/5 oz/10 tbsp butter
grated rind of 1 orange
about 60 ml/4 tbsp ice cold water
225 g/8 oz/1½ cups vegetarian
   mincemeat
1 beaten egg, to glaze
icing sugar, to dust

1 Sift together the flour, icing sugar and cinnamon then rub in the butter until it forms crumbs. (This can be done in a food processor.) Stir in the grated orange rind.

2 Mix to a firm dough with the ice cold water. Knead lightly, then roll out to a 5 mm/¼ in thickness.

3 Using a 7 cm/2½ in round cutter, cut out 18 circles, re-rolling as necessary. Then cut out 18 smaller 5 cm/2 in circles. If liked, cut out little shapes from the centre of the smaller circles.

4 Line two bun tins with the 18 larger circles – they will fill one and a half tins. Spoon a small spoonful of mincemeat into each pastry case and top with the smaller pastry circles, pressing the edges lightly together to seal.

5 Glaze the tops of the pies with egg and leave to rest in the refrigerator for 30 minutes. Preheat the oven to 200°C/400°F/Gas 6.

6 Bake the pies for 15–20 minutes until they are golden brown. Remove them to wire racks to cool. Serve just warm and dusted with icing sugar.

Christmas Pudding

If possible, try to make your puddings at least one month before Christmas for the flavours to develop and mature. Dried prunes and apricots add an unusual texture and delicious flavour to this recipe.

MAKES TWO 1 LITRE/2 PINT PUDDINGS
275 g/10 oz/5 cups fresh white
  breadcrumbs
225 g/8 oz/2 cups shredded vegetarian
  suet or ice cold butter, coarsely grated
115 g/4 oz/1 cup plain flour
225 g/8 oz/1 cup soft brown sugar
10 ml/2 tsp ground mixed spice
350 g/12 oz/2½ cups currants
350 g/12 oz/2½ cups raisins
225 g/8 oz/1¾ cups sultanas
150 g/6 oz/1 cup stoned no-need-to-soak
  prunes, chopped
115 g/4 oz/¾ cup no-need-to-soak dried
  apricots, chopped
115 g/4 oz/¾ cup candied peel, chopped
115 g/4 oz/¾ cup glacé cherries, washed
  and chopped
rind of 1 large lemon, grated
4 eggs, beaten
30 ml/2 tbsp black treacle
150 ml/¼ pint/⅔ cup beer or milk
60 ml/4 tbsp brandy or rum

1 Grease two 1 litre/2 pint pudding basins and line the bases with small discs of greaseproof paper.

2 Mix all the ingredients together well. If you intend to put lucky coins or tokens in the mixture, boil them first to ensure they are clean and wrap them in foil.

3 Pack the mixture into the two basins, pushing it down lightly.

4 Cover each pudding with greased greaseproof paper and a double thickness of foil. Secure it round the rim with kitchen string.

5 Place two old china saucers in the base of two large saucepans. Stand the basins on the saucers, pour boiling water to come two thirds of the way up and boil gently for about 6 hours, checking the water level regularly and topping it up with more boiling water.

6 When cooked, cool the puddings, remove the foil and paper then re-cover to store. On Christmas Day, re-boil for about 2 hours and serve with brandy butter and cream or custard.

Index

Acknowledgements

Alcan Consumer Products,
Raans Rd,
Amersham,
Bucks. HP6 6JY
Tel: 01494 721261

Bridgewater China
739 Fulham Road
London SW6
Tel: 0171 371 9033

Corning Consumer Ltd

Le Creuset supplied by
The Kitchenware Merchants Ltd,
4 Stephenson Close,
East Portway,
Andover,
Hampshire SP10 3RU
Tel: 0800 373792

The Denby Pottery Company Ltd,
Denby,
Derbyshire,
DE5 8NX
Tel: 01773 743641

Gas hob supplied by
Worldpool UK Ltd,
PO Box 45, 209 Purley Way,
Croydon CR9 4RY
Tel: 0181 649 5000

Kenwood Appliances,
New Lane,
Havant,
Hants. PO9 2NH
Tel: 01705 476000

Lakeland Plastics Ltd,
Alexandra Buildings,
Windermere,
Cumbria LA23 1BQ
Tel: 015394 88100

Oneida Silversmiths,
Pembroke House,
Pembroke Road,
Ruislip,
Middlesex HA4 8NQ
Tel: 01895 639452

Prestige Group UK plc,
P.O. Box 95,
Colne Road,
Burnley,
Lancs. BB11 2AB
Tel: 01282 830101

Tefal UK Ltd, to find local stockists:
Tel: Customer Services 01604 762726

Victorinox Swiss Cutlery UK Ltd,
Victorinox House,
163 Parker Drive,
Leicester LE4 0JP
Tel: 01533 351111